The Concise Guide to
Digital Photography

igloobooks

Published in 2014
by Igloo Books Ltd
Cottage Farm
Sywell
NN6 0BJ
www.igloobooks.com

Copyright© 2014 Igloo Books Ltd

All content and images supplied by

Bauer Media / Practical Photography
10-13, 52-53, 86-93, 114-128

© What Digital Camera / IPC+ Syndication
14-43, 46-51, 54-69, 72-83, 94-97, 100-111

The following images are courtesy of Thinkstock
82, 83, 87 (both), 101 (l), 114, 115, 116 (main), 117, 118, 119, 120, 121

HUN001 0214
2 4 6 8 10 9 7 5 3 1
ISBN 978-1-78197-067-6

Printed and manufactured in China

The Concise Guide to
Digital Photography

CONTENTS

INTRODUCTION

Photography can be incredibly rewarding, especially if the results are a testament to weeks of devoted practice and perseverance. Understanding your camera takes time, and much of it can be attributed to experience and confidence as well as knowing the technicalities of your equipment.

This step-by-step guide aims to debunk the processes behind what some regard as their hobby, and others a vocation. The chapters are arranged into six handy stages, each targeting a specific area that will enhance your learning, and enable you to see the bigger picture! These are: Fundamentals of Photography, Choosing and Using Your Kit, Understanding Your Camera, Landscapes, Portraits and Photo Projects.

This book is a great tool for both amateurs and professionals alike.

It provides vital information that is truly accessible to all eager learners. The Glossary is a fantastic resource which features all of the ingredients needed to master the art of photography. You'll soon be a pro once you add the likes of "aperture" and "white balance" to your vocabulary!

Dotted throughout are colourful images which demonstrate the dos and don'ts for each mode and setting. These are accompanied by useful hints and tips, so you'll be well on your way to producing that award-winning glossy picture.

Feel free to dip in and out as you please, at your own leisurely pace. There are no rules here! After all, photography should be a fun, creative experience.

And remember: sometimes the best shots are born from a surge of spontaneity.

CHAPTER ONE

FUNDAMENTALS
OF PHOTOGRAPHY »

GLOSSARY

JUST BOUGHT YOUR FIRST CAMERA BUT TOO EMBARRASSED TO ASK WHAT THE BASIC PHOTOGRAPHIC TERMS MEAN? YOU'VE COME TO THE RIGHT PLACE – WE'RE HERE TO HELP!

APERTURE

is the variable opening inside a lens that governs how much light passes to the sensor. It works in conjunction with the shutter and metering system to produce exposures. Apertures are known as f/numbers or f/stops. These are commonly arranged as f/2.8, f/4, f/5.6, f/8, f/11, f/16 and f/22, with f/2.8 letting in the most light and f/22 the least.

CAMERA SHAKE

occurs when movement of the camera is recorded in the final image. It's most common when using long exposures and focal lengths. As a rule of thumb try to use a shutter speed of at least 1/focal length to minimise camera shake, ie if you're using a 200mm lens use a shutter speed of 1/200sec or faster, such as 1/250sec or 1/500sec.

COMPOSITION

literally means 'putting together' and is the term used to describe the placement or arrangement of objects in a photograph. Lens choice, framing, focal point, depth-of-field, lighting, line, shape, colour, texture, form and space all contribute to composition, as do traditional techniques such as the rule-of-thirds, lead-in lines and foreground interest.

DEPTH-OF-FIELD

is the amount of the image that's sharp from near to far. It's governed by the focal length of the lens, the aperture used and the distance between you and the object that you've focused on. To achieve the most depth-of-field use a wide-angle lens and a small aperture (f/16 to f/32). The longer the focal length of the lens and the wider the aperture you use, the shallower the depth-of-field becomes.

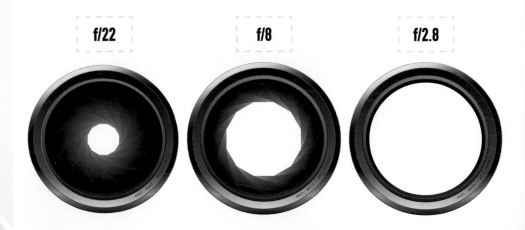

f/22   f/8   f/2.8

SHALLOW DEPTH-OF-FIELD

F/2.8

LARGE DEPTH-OF-FIELD

F/22

Underexposed 1/250sec @ f/5.6

Correctly exposed 1/60sec @ f/5.6

EXPOSURE is a measure of the total amount of light that's allowed to fall on a digital sensor during the recording of a photograph. The exposure time is determined by the duration of the shutter opening (referred to as the shutter speed), and the level of illumination received by the sensor is determined by the size of the opening in the lens iris (referred to as the aperture).

Overexposure occurs when too much light hits the sensor, resulting in light images with little or no detail in the highlights. Overexposure is the result of an inappropriate exposure being set, either automatically by the camera or manually by the photographer.

Underexposure occurs when not enough light has passed to the sensor, resulting in a dark image with little or no shadow detail. Underexposure is the result of an inappropriate exposure being set, either automatically by the camera or manually by the photographer.

HISTOGRAMS are bar charts that show the brightness levels of a picture. They range from blacks/shadows on the left, through midtones in the centre, to whites/highlights on the right. Histograms can be found on a camera's LCD, in RAW software and in Photoshop. In-camera histograms can be useful when assessing your images for overexposure and underexposure.

ISO is a way of controlling the sensitivity of a camera's sensor to light. The most common settings are ISO 100, 200, 400, 800 and 1600. The higher the number the more sensitive the sensor is to light, allowing you to shoot in darker conditions. So for bright conditions you can use a low ISO such as 100 or 200, and in darker conditions you'll need a higher ISO of 400 or above.

JPEG is a widely used digital file type that compresses the information from a photo into a relatively small file. The compression allows the file to use less memory but it also loses a certain amount of quality in the process. As such it is known as a lossy file. Every time you save a JPEG it gets more compressed, which means that the picture is losing more detail with each save. Digital cameras allow you to choose JPEG quality. JPEG stands for Joint Photographic Experts Group.

MEGAPIXELS (MP) equal one million pixels and refer to the number of image sensors on a camera's CCD or CMOS sensor. For example, a camera with an array of 6000x4000 pixels on its sensor is described as a 24MP (6000 x 4000 = 24,000,000) camera. The term megapixel can also be used to describe the number of pixels in an image, or the number of display elements of digital displays, such as a computer monitor.

GLOSSARY

METERING

Metering systems measure the amount of light entering the camera through the lens (TTL) and then translate this information into shutter speed and aperture values. DSLRs feature several different metering modes:

Evaluative/Matrix: The default mode where exposure readings are taken from across the entire length and width of the frame, and calculated into one 'average' exposure.

Centre-weighted/ Average: Most of the exposure is taken from the centre of the frame, but the surrounding areas are also factored into the reading.

Spot/Partial: The exposure is taken from a small area in the centre of the frame (or selected AF point) and is ideal for backlit subjects.

RAW is a digital file type where the data is taken directly from the sensor. Unlike other file types, no image processing is performed in-camera, so you have to process them once downloaded to your computer. This makes RAW files more versatile than their JPEG counterparts, as you can change the settings from those chosen when you shot the image without any loss in quality. The downsides are that it takes time to process the images and they can't be successfully printed directly from the camera.

RESOLUTION relates directly to image quality. Images are made up of millions of tiny blocks of colour called pixels – more pixels means smaller pixels and this in turn means smoother detail. The number and size of the pixels determines the size an image can be printed without individual pixels being visible to the naked eye. Large pixels equals low resolution and small pixels equals high resolution. The term pixels per inch (ppi) is often used when sizing images – 300ppi is the generally accepted optimum resolution for printing.

SENSORS are silicon-based devices that convert light into electronic signals. Sensors consist of millions of photosensitive diodes (known as photosites) that relay pixels to the camera's memory card as image files. These files can then be viewed on the LCD screen. There are two types of sensors – CCD and CMOS. CCD (Charged Coupling Device) sensors offer high quality/low noise images, but the technology is now over 30

years old. CMOS (Complimentary Metal Oxide Semiconductor) sensors are cheaper and more energy-efficient, but are prone to noise.

SHUTTER SPEED refers to the amount of time the shutter is open in order to allow light to fall on the sensor and record an exposure. It's measured in a fraction of, or multiple of, a whole second, ie 1/125sec and 2 seconds. Used in conjunction with the aperture, it helps control image exposure. Also, the longer the focal length, the faster the shutter speed needed to shoot handheld and capture sharp shots.

VIEWFINDERS are the small windows you look through in cameras to compose your images. DSLR viewfinders display the exact same image that will be captured on the sensor. Most compacts also have a viewfinder but these are adjacent to the lens and you don't see the exact image that will be captured. Check to see what percentage of the actual image they show.

WHITE BALANCE (often referred to as WB) is the process of correcting unwanted colour casts so results are neutral. Digital cameras use a WB system to compensate for the varying colour temperatures from different light sources. This light varies in colour from the warm orange/red of normal light bulbs to the more blue light of bright, overcast daylight. The auto white balance setting tries to interpret the colours to give neutral results, and there are manual settings that give pre-set values to the colours.

IN DETAIL: PRIME LENSES

A prime is any lens with a fixed focal length. Though less versatile than zooms, which have variable focal lengths, prime lenses benefit from being smaller, lighter and, quite often, sharper. They contain fewer moving parts and fewer elements (the actual glass components), resulting in larger maximum apertures, such as f/2.8, f/1.8 and even f/1.4. As such, they're perfect for working in low light conditions and for creating extreme shallow depth-of-field effects. Popular prime lens focal lengths include 28mm, 35mm, 50mm, 85mm, 100mm and 300mm. 50mm primes are often referred to as standard lenses, as the focal length is roughly the same as that of a human eye when the lens is used on a film SLR or full-frame DSLR.

There are numerous primes for all needs and budgets.

IN DETAIL: DRIVE MODES

All DSLRs and CSCs feature three standard drive modes – single shot, continuous and self-timer. These can be accessed either via the top-plate (pictured), or the mode dial or menu. Single shot does exactly what it says on the tin – you press the shutter button and the camera will take one shot. Continuous mode allows you to shoot two or more frames in quick succession, with the frames-per-second (fps) shooting speed varying from around 3.5fps for entry-level cameras to around 8fps for semi-pro models. Self-timer gives a 2-second or 10-second delay between the shutter being pressed and the exposure being taken. More advanced models might offer drive modes such as silent, mirror-up and wireless control.

FOCUSING

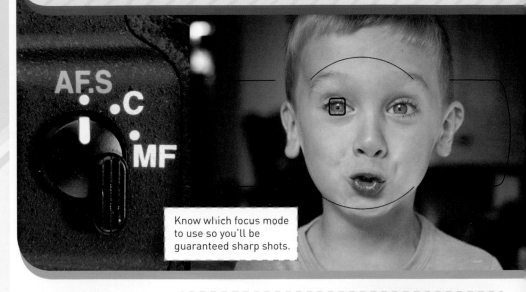

Know which focus mode to use so you'll be guaranteed sharp shots.

ENSURE PIN-SHARP SHOTS BY UNDERSTANDING YOUR CAMERA'S FOCUSING MODES

Focusing is one of the key cornerstones of photography, with pin-sharp images the desired aesthetic for most people.

Autofocus has made achieving this much easier for many, but as technology has seen AF become increasingly sophisticated with more modes available, it has become ever more important for you to know which mode to select for the subject you're photographing. Here are the key focusing modes that you need to know...

FOCUS MODES EXPLAINED

SINGLE AF

SINGLE

Single AF, often referred to as AF-S or One Shot, is ideal for shooting general and static subjects. Once you have half-depressed the shutter button, the camera acquires focus, so if your subject moves, you will have to re-focus – but for static subjects, this won't be an issue.

CONTINUOUS

If your subject is likely to move when you're shooting, choose Continuous AF, which is labelled AF-C or AI Servo for Canon users. As you half-depress the shutter button, the camera will continue to adjust focus on the subject until you fire the shutter, ensuring focus is maintained.

CONTINUOUS AF

AUTO

Not every camera will have this AF mode, but in essence, it's a combination of single-shot and continuous AF modes. Termed AF-A or AI Focus, the camera will initially be in single-shot mode, but should your subject move, it will automatically swap to continuous AF to ensure your shot remains sharp.

AUTO AF

FOCUS TRACKING

While continuous AF will adjust focus on a single point, Focus Tracking is clever enough to track the subject as it moves across the frame. Some systems offer a plethora of custom settings to fine-tune depending on how erratically and fast you anticipate your subject to be moving.

FOCUS

MANUAL

There will be times when you'll need to focus manually, such as when you're photographing close-up macro subjects and want to be very precise with your point of focus. Other scenarios where MF will be useful is when you want to focus on a specific point when you're taking multiple shots.

MANUAL FOCUS

SHUTTER SPEED

Fast shutter speeds are ideal for freezing action.

THE SHUTTER SPEED DETERMINES THE LENGTH OF YOUR EXPOSURE TIME, AND AFFECTS THE WAY THAT MOTION IS RECORDED BY YOUR CAMERA

The shutter speed is, along with the aperture, one of the two primary controls available to adjust the amount of light that reaches the sensor. But while the aperture controls the intensity of light, the shutter speed determines the duration for which the sensor is exposed to it.

To compare a camera with an oven, the aperture represents the temperature, and the shutter speed is akin to the cooking time. Creating a perfect picture, just like cooking a perfect pie, involves getting the right combination of these two controls.

CONTROLLING EXPOSURE

Longer shutter speeds allow more light to reach the sensor; short ones allow less light to pass.

The lower the prevailing light level, the longer the shutter needs to remain open in order to record a correctly exposed shot. Just like the aperture, the shutter speed range is measured in stops, with each stop doubling or halving the exposure value. Unlike apertures though, the numerical relationship is more obvious. So a speed of 1/2000sec lets in half the amount of light of 1/1000sec, but double that of 1/4000sec.

TRACKING YOUR SUBJECT'S MOTION WHILE USING A SLOWER SHUTTER SPEED (PANNING) CREATES A MOTION-BLURRED BACKGROUND WHICH CONVEYS A SENSE OF 'SPEED'.

SHUTTER SPEED SCALE

The shutter speed range available on a camera varies: top of the range DSLRs may offer speeds from 1/8000sec to 30 seconds. In addition there will be a setting called 'B' in which the shutter will stay open for as long as you hold it down (or locked open using a remote release), which is ideal for night photography. Compact cameras have a much shorter range of speeds.

FASTER SPEEDS *LESS LIGHT*

1/8000
1/4000
1/2000
1/1000
1/500
1/250
1/125
1/60
1/30
1/15
1/8
¼
½
1sec
2secs
4secs
8secs

SLOWER SPEEDS *MORE LIGHT*

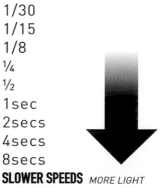

SHUTTER SPEED

AVOID CAMERA SHAKE

Your shutter speed choice also affects the overall sharpness of your image. You may not be aware of it, but the natural movement in your hands transfers to the picture, resulting in camera shake. The degree of shake varies depending on many factors and it may not be visible till you enlarge the shot. The more telephoto your lens, the greater this problem is magnified, so to reduce the risks, a good rule of thumb is to ensure that your shutter speed is at least equal to the focal length of the lens. So if you're using an 18-55mm lens at the 55mm end, don't let the speed go below 1/60sec, and if you're using a 200mm lens, keep it to 1/250 or above. If there isn't enough light to use these speeds, raise the ISO or use a tripod.

FREEZING MOTION

Shutter speeds have a profound effect on how the camera records moving subjects. A fast shutter speed stops fast motion in its tracks as though the subject is frozen in time. You've all seen shots of high jumpers suspended in mid-air above the bar. That's done with fast shutter speeds.

BLURRING MOTION

Using slower speeds will cause some motion blur but this may be desirable. A racing car 'frozen' on the track will look like it's parked, whereas a speed that allows a controlled amount of subject blur will better convey its motion.

PANNING

One useful technique employed by many sports photographers is to move the camera with the subject, keeping it in the same position in the frame. This is known as panning, and the effect is to keep the subject relatively sharp but blur the background with streaking. The precise speeds to use vary depending on your subject, and the effect desired, so you'll need to experiment.

THE SLOWER THE SHUTTER SPEED, THE GREATER THE MOTION BLUR YOU WILL RECORD

1/250th

1/60th

1/15th

METERING

CONFUSED BY THE TERM METERING?
HERE WE MAKE IT EASIER FOR YOU TO UNDERSTAND

The term metering comes from the good old-fashioned light meter: a device used to measure the intensity of light to provide photographers with a better understanding of which camera settings result in a correctly exposed image. Thanks to advances in modern technology, metering systems are now featured within all digital cameras, while on a majority of Compact System Cameras and DSLRs, you're given precise control of how the metering system works. In addition to different metering modes, exposure compensation can be used to override what the camera's metering system thinks is the perfect exposure. Over these pages we'll study the differences between metering modes, show you how exposure lock can be activated and explain what exposure compensation really is.

MOST CAMERAS GIVE YOU THE OPTION TO CHANGE METERING MODE TO MAKE IT SUITABLE FOR YOUR SHOOTING SITUATION.

METERING MODES EXPLAINED

EVALUATIVE

Of the four metering modes that a DSLR will typically offer, Evaluative is possibly the most sophisticated. Also known as Matrix metering, it studies the entire scene you're photographing rather than a specific point in the frame. The advantage of using Evaluative metering is that the camera uses its complicated algorithms to study the scene or the subject you're shooting before automatically setting the best metering to suit. If you're unsure of which metering mode to use, Evaluative is the safest option and it'll allow you to concentrate on other important fundamentals such as framing and composition.

PARTIAL

Partial metering is found on most cameras and is good to use when attempting to photograph backlit subjects. A great example is an outdoor portrait with the light shining from behind. Rather than metering the entire scene, which could result in the face appearing dark against the background, Partial metering is weighted towards the centre of the frame. The result of using this mode will be correctly exposed skin tones, with a background that appears lighter and brighter. Try using this mode when you have a specific area of a photograph that you'd like the exposure to be based on.

EXPOSURE COMPENSATION

Most of the time we rely on a camera's metering system to do all the hard work for us, but there will be times when we take an image only to find the end result appears lighter or darker than we viewed it with our own eyes at the point of capture. The truth is, camera metering systems can be fooled in tricky lighting conditions –

an example being a predominantly light scene such as a snow scene. Metering systems do tend to underexpose in these types of situations and one way to get around the problem is to dial in a few stops of exposure compensation.

Exposure compensation is a feature found on most types of camera and

SPOT

Spot metering is equivalent to the Partial metering mode you'll find on other cameras. Essentially, both these modes do exactly the same job and, just like Partial metering, Spot metering should be used when you want to ensure a specific area or subject in the frame is correctly exposed. On some more advanced cameras you'll find that the Spot metering is linked to the AF points. On most cameras though, Spot metering is linked to the central AF point only. This means you'll be required to move the target over your subject to take your exposure reading before then recomposing your shot.

CENTRE-WEIGHTED

Centre-weighted is a metering mode that gives priority to the centre portion of the photograph, but also takes the surrounding areas of the image into consideration. It could be looked at as being a halfway house in-between Evaluative metering and Partial/Spot metering modes. If you regularly shoot subjects that are composed in the centre of the frame but are not covered by the centre AF target, it's a good metering mode to use. With Centre-weighted selected, the camera will take its metering information from various points around the frame but will dedicate more weight to those in the middle.

allows the user to adjust the automatically calculated exposure so it appears brighter or darker than what the metering system thinks is right. Compensation is controlled by entering a positive or negative value into the camera and is controlled in stops, half stops, and up to a third of a stop on some advanced cameras. If your results

from using the camera's metering system appear too dark and you'd like a lighter result, you'll want to dial in a positive value such as +2EV. Alternatively, if your image seems too dark you can enter a negative value such as -2EV, which will have the opposite effect.

ISO

YOUR CAMERA'S SENSITIVITY CAN MAKE ALL THE DIFFERENCE WHEN CAPTURING THAT CRUCIAL IMAGE

The sensor inside your digital camera is designed to work within a whole range of lighting conditions, and it's here where knowing about your camera's ISO settings comes in handy. Taking control of your camera's ISO – which regulates its sensitivity to light – allows you to choose the most appropriate option for the scene in hand. By doing so, you can ensure that images captured in good light retain excellent image quality, while those captured in sub-optimum conditions still emerge sharp and full of detail. Problems arise at higher sensitivities where the camera tries to produce the best images it can with the light available, and also at longer exposures, but the good news is that your camera will typically have tools at its disposal to counter these effects. So, what options are there, and exactly when should you use them?

ISO SETTINGS

EXPLAINED

ISO 100-400

Where possible you should try to stick to low settings as they will create the least image noise. In poorer lighting conditions though, you may find the shutter speed to be too slow; in this case, you should select a wider aperture or increase the ISO setting.

ISO 800-1600

This range is particularly useful when capturing action, as it has the effect of raising the shutter speed while keeping image noise to a minimum. You may also need to use such settings outdoors in the early evening and indoors when shooting under moderate light.

ISO 3200-6400

These settings should be used when lower ISO settings fail to provide a high enough shutter speed, although they will create more noise than lower ISOs. Typical candidates for this range include darker interiors and night-time street scenes.

ISO 12,800+

Settings at ISO 12,800 and above should be used as a last resort, as they create the most noise. The most suitable subjects are those with the least ambient light: most scenes outdoors at night, as well as dimly lit interiors and live music events all fall into this category.

YOUR CAMERA SHOULD ALLOW SENSITIVITY TO BE ADJUSTED FROM AROUND ISO 100 TO AS MUCH AS ISO 12,800 OR MORE.

AUTO ISO

MOST CAMERAS NOW HAVE AN AUTO ISO OPTION, WHICH TAKES THE HARD WORK OUT OF DECIDING WHICH SETTING TO USE.

If you're not sure which ISO setting is the most appropriate in a given situation, fear not – the chances are your camera can decide this for you. Many cameras now have an "Auto ISO" setting to do this, and some more advanced models can have the extent of the range determined by the photographer. By doing this, some of the highest few sensitivities – i.e. those which will produce the most noise – will be avoided. So does the camera always get it right? Obviously this varies from camera to camera, although for the most part the camera will simply pick the lowest sensitivity that will produce an acceptably sharp image, which is largely determined by the focal length of the lens in use. The camera won't, however, take any subject movement into consideration when deciding this value, which means that there is a chance the camera can still capture an image with some blur if your subject is moving. Some cameras do have the ability to sense motion, and adjust the shutter speed accordingly, but many do not; in this instance, you may stand a better chance of capturing an image sharply by setting the camera to its Shutter Priority setting and choosing a shutter speed fast enough to freeze movement – around 1/250sec and upwards – while using the Auto ISO option. This will then determine both the appropriate ISO value and aperture to enable that shutter speed to be used.

HIGH ISO NOISE REDUCTION

LONG EXPOSURE NOISE REDUCTION

NOISE REDUCTION

DSLRs, Compact System Cameras and an increasing number of compact cameras now have the option of applying noise reduction to images. Typically this is offered for two separate types of images: those captured at higher sensitivities and particularly long exposures. The two work in different ways, given the type of noise created in each. Noise reduction applied to high-sensitivity images is usually offered in low, medium and strong options. As a lot of the noise these settings attempt to reduce is random in nature, these work on the image as a whole, which means they tend to also affect details which are not visibly affected by noise. Therefore, the strongest settings will indeed have the effect of removing the most noise, but at the expense of detail. If you plan on enlarging your images, or cropping into them heavily in post-production, you may, therefore, prefer to use a low or medium setting, or alternatively capture a Raw image and process it later when you have more time to get the result you want in post-production.

Long exposure noise reduction works in a different way. Much of the noise which forms during a long exposure can be measured more accurately by a camera, and so it can be removed more effectively by noise reduction. The camera will typically calculate where on the sensor this noise forms from a subsequent image taken without any exposure to light. It then subtracts that noise from the original image, leaving the details in the image largely unaffected. It is, therefore, recommended when shooting long exposures.

DIRECTION OF LIGHT

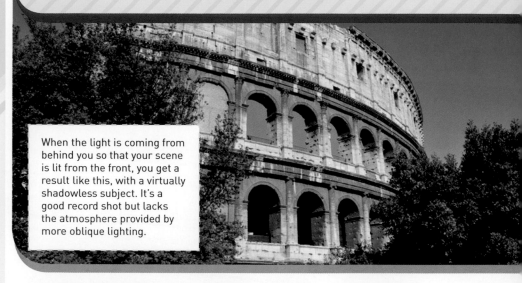

When the light is coming from behind you so that your scene is lit from the front, you get a result like this, with a virtually shadowless subject. It's a good record shot but lacks the atmosphere provided by more oblique lighting.

IT'S NOT JUST HOW MUCH LIGHT YOU'VE GOT THAT COUNTS — THE DIRECTION THAT THE LIGHT IS COMING FROM HAS A PROFOUND EFFECT ON THE FINAL IMAGE

One of the most important factors in the quality of light is the direction from which it's coming. A commonly quoted rule of thumb is to shoot with the sun behind you so that it lights the front of your subject.

There's nothing wrong with that. You'll get an evenly lit record of your subject and maybe even a nice blue sky in the background, but this kind of light is a little flat and two-dimensional, and less interesting from a photographer's point of view. It's better when the light is oblique, and casts shadows.

SIDELIGHTING

When a subject is lit from the side two things happen. Firstly, parts of the scene go in to shade, and it's this mix of light and shade that make a picture look more three-dimensional and interesting. The second thing that happens is you can suddenly start to see the texture in your subject, whether in brickwork, wood, even people's faces (which may not always be a good thing!).

You can create this texture even on a small scale in a home studio by placing a

hard, high-contrast light source to the side of your subject so that it glances across its surface.

CONTRE JOUR

Shooting directly into the light can sometimes produce the most compelling shots. Long shadows extend towards the camera and subjects can take on an attractive halo around their edges, which can be very flattering with portraits, when the hair becomes backlit.

These two images were taken within five minutes of each other. The key difference is the direction of the light. In the first shot (left) the sun is behind and to the right of the camera. The second image (right) was taken from the other side of the building, shooting directly into the light and metering from the sky to render the subject as a silhouette.

Setting the right exposure, however, can be tricky, because the front of your subject will be in deep shadow, so depending on where you take your meter reading you'll get a very different result.

If you want the front of the subject to be exposed correctly you'll need to either take a selective reading from this area, excluding the light coming from behind, and thus over-exposing the background, or you'll have to add light to the front to fill in the shadows – either from a reflector or additional lighting.

On the other hand you could choose to set your exposure for the brightly lit background and turn your subject into a silhouette (see top right). This method can work well if your subject has an interesting outline that would look good as a silhouette. If its outline is a rectangular slab then obviously it won't.

SIDELIGHTING CASTS DEEP SHADOWS AND REVEALS THE TEXTURES ON THE SURFACES OF YOUR SUBJECT, AS IN THIS EXAMPLE TAKEN AT RED ROCK CANYON, NEVADA.

VIEWPOINT

DON'T SETTLE FOR THE MOST OBVIOUS AND FAMILIAR VIEWS OF WELL-KNOWN SUBJECTS. SEEK OUT MORE INTERESTING AND UNUSUAL ALTERNATIVES

One of the commonest mistakes that many people make in pictorial photography is to shoot from where they happen to be standing when they see whatever it is that they want to photograph. More often than not, a better picture can be found by walking around and exploring alternative viewpoints.

Before you press that shutter button, pause for a moment and take a breath. Take a good look at the subject you're about to photograph, and then at the area around it.

Ask yourself a few questions: Is this the best position to shoot from? Am I close enough, or would I get more impact by getting closer still? Have I got the best lens on the camera for this subject, or would a longer or shorter focal length work better? How is the light falling on the subject from this position? Would the composition or lighting look better if I moved further to the left or the right? What does the subject look like from the other side?

The Taj Mahal is one of the most photographed buildings in the world. Everyone shoots in from the entrance, and the iconic shot from the end of the reflecting pool, but there are lots of other angles. These pictures are a small selection from a larger set taken during a period of about three hours.

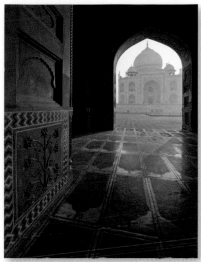 

By all means take the shot you saw first, but once you've got the first shot in the bag take a bit of time to explore other possibilities. After all, if a subject is worth photographing it's worth spending more than just a couple of seconds on it. This especially holds true for subjects, locations and landmarks that you may have taken a lot of trouble to get to.

Don't be afraid to take lots of pictures, especially if you're shooting handheld. If you're planning to shoot a more considered landscape scene, using a tripod, at least walk around to pick the best spot before setting up. If you're aiming to photograph, say, a landscape at sunset, get there in enough time to have explored every possible viewpoint before the crucial time, so you can be confident that when you open up your tripod you're in the best spot.

SHADOWS AND REFLECTIONS

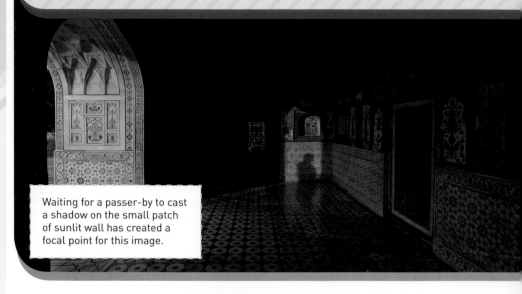

Waiting for a passer-by to cast a shadow on the small patch of sunlit wall has created a focal point for this image.

INTERESTING SHADOWS AND REFLECTIONS CAN ENHANCE THE MOOD OF YOUR SCENE, AND OFFER THE POTENTIAL FOR GREAT ABSTRACT SHOTS

Some of the most interesting photography is not of objects, but of light, and the way it falls upon the things around us. Shadows are among the most photogenic of subjects, whether you include the object that's casting it or just focus on the shadow itself. In order to get interesting shadows you do need a sunny day, but it's much better to shoot in the early morning or late afternoon when the sun is lower and the shadows longer. Winter is a great season to shoot because the sun is lower in the sky anyway. Most of the best opportunities come when you're shooting into the sun or it's coming from the side. When it's behind you the biggest challenge is keeping your own shadow out of the shot.

Most camera exposure meters are well able to cope with abstract shadows but to get maximum impact try taking a selective reading from a sunlit area so that the shadow records a deep black.

A man relaxing at a seafront cafe casts a giant shadow on the windbreak in this contre-jour shot taken in Hove.

REFLECTIONS

Photographing reflections is like a 'two for the price of one' deal – you get not only the subject but the reflection of it too. This is one of the few occasions where it's okay to put the horizon across the middle of the frame, or alternatively you can give more prominence to the reflection or its source by moving the horizon up or down in the frame. In fact you can exclude the subject altogether if you like and just photograph the reflection. Some people like to turn the resulting images upside down to fool the viewer into thinking it's a slightly surreal image of the object itself.

Reflections don't have to be of large subjects such as buildings either. Wet pavements provide the perfect opportunity to photograph the reflections of street lights on the slabs, or in puddles.

The landscaped gardens of the Taj Mahal feature a reflecting pool. Here the Taj itself has been excluded from the shot, leaving only its reflection, to create an abstract image.

SUNSET IS A GREAT TIME TO PHOTOGRAPH SUBJECTS REFLECTED IN WATER, AS IT DOUBLES THE IMPACT.

COLOUR AND TEXTURE

PICTURES DON'T HAVE TO BE ABOUT THINGS; THEY CAN BE ABOUT THE QUALITIES OF THOSE THINGS, SUCH AS THEIR COLOUR AND TEXTURE. HERE ARE A FEW TIPS

This isn't a picture of a plant pot. Well, it is – but that isn't the subject. It's about the contrast between the yellow of the pot and the rich blue background. The strong shapes and shadows add to the appeal. Shot in Marrakesh, Morocco.

Sometimes the most striking thing about a scene is its colour, or the colour of an object within it. There are many ways in which colour can be used as the subject itself. It may just be a very colourful scene, such as a group of Indian women in colourful saris. But it often works better if there is a dominance of a single colour. Buddhist monks all wearing the same saffron robes, for example.

Sometimes an image can be entirely monochromatic in that it is all different shades and hues of one colour, and this can also be very powerful. Another visual device that works well is when the image is all one colour but with an accent of a contrasting colour. An example might be a bright yellow kite against a deep blue sky, or a single lime in a big bowl of oranges.

It's important to remember that light has its own colour, which means that you can also base compositions around the mixed colours of ambient light, though you'll need a good understanding of how your white balance works. For example, if you encounter a scene that includes both daylight and artificial tungsten light you can choose to set the white balance for the daylight, or the tungsten light, which will give you a different result in each case.

Complementary colours work especially well to provide contrasting compositions, such as blue and yellow, red and turquoise, or green and pink.

This image offers both colour and texture. The colour, and smooth shiny surface of the beer can, contrasts with the subdued hues and bumpy texture of the pebbles on the beach.

TEXTURE

There's lots of photographic potential to be had from photographing the texture of things, whether they be natural or man-made. Texture is accentuated with strong, hard sidelighting, so for example a low direct sun skimming across a landscape will accentuate the texture in the grass and rocks. Light glancing across a tree will enhance the texture of the bark, and make the veins in the leaves stand out.

You can easily create your own hard sidelighting to accentuate the texture of still-life subjects in your home. An angle-poise lamp, with its small direct light source, is all you need. Position it so that the light falls across the surface of your subject from an oblique angle.

Another image that depends on colour contrast, this time between red and green, with the additional appeal of strong shadows falling over the doorway.

BLACK AND WHITE

MANY OF THE MOST MEMORABLE IMAGES OF ALL TIME ARE BLACK AND WHITE, AND WITH GOOD REASON. AND IN THE AGE OF DIGITAL IT'S AS POPULAR AS EVER

Cities are a great subject for black and white because there often isn't much colour anyway. Grey, overcast days in particular generally work better in mono.

Despite the fact that colour photography has been with us for over a century, black and white still refuses to go away, and in fact has seen a resurgence in popularity in recent years. This is perhaps because it has a purity that colour lacks. With some subjects the colour can actually be a distraction from the message or story you're trying to convey, and stripping it away brings that story to the fore.

This is one reason why black and white photography is still so popular among photojournalists and social documentary photographers. Many portrait photographers swear that black and white images seem to get closer to the soul of the person, and for landscape photographers black and white is the perfect solution when shooting on a grey, drab and colourless day. Finally, ironically, black and white photographs don't tend

to date as badly as colour. Sceptical? Just look at classic colour photographs from the past 50 years and compare them with black and white images from the same period.

SHOOTING IN B&W

Without colour, black and white photography depends more on other compositional devices for its artistic impact: qualities such as shape and form, texture, tone and contrast. Some of the graphical devices discussed already such as leading lines can be even more powerful.

One of the most difficult skills to learn when shooting black and white is how to see a coloured world in grey tones. Scenes that may work well in colour will fail in black and white if the colours reproduce as similar shades of grey.

Setting your camera to black and white, or monochrome mode, can help you with this visualisation but don't rely on the black and white jpeg as your final image. There's a huge variety of custom tonal adjustment you can make on your PC if you convert a colour image to mono, and the result will be far better.

So make sure you shoot in raw+jpeg mode so you get a black and white jpeg for visual reference in the field, but a full colour Raw file to work on when you get back to your computer.

The strong graphic lines, and contrast between the flagpoles and deep blue sky were a natural subject for the b&w treatment.

TEXTURE AND DETAIL COME TO THE FORE WHEN COLOUR IS REMOVED FROM THE IMAGE, AS IN THIS SHOT OF A FISHING BOAT.

The strong graphic contrast and long, deep shadows in this Rome street scene make the image look like a scene out of *La Dolce Vita* when converted to black and white.

MOVEMENT

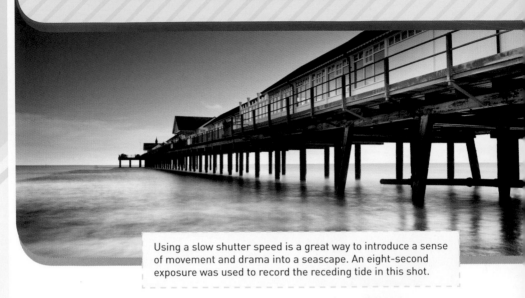

Using a slow shutter speed is a great way to introduce a sense of movement and drama into a seascape. An eight-second exposure was used to record the receding tide in this shot.

THE SHUTTER PRIORITY MODE IS THE BEST ONE TO CHOOSE FOR MOVING SUBJECTS, AS IT LETS YOU CHOOSE HOW YOU WANT TO RECORD THE MOTION IN YOUR IMAGE

If the subject that you're trying to photograph is moving it's time to switch to Shutter Priority and think about how you want that motion to be recorded. It could be that you want to freeze the motion so that it's sharp, in which case you need to set a shutter speed high enough to achieve this. The precise speed you'll need to use will depend on many factors, not least of which is the speed of the subject, but will also factor other variables such as its distance from the camera and size within the frame. If the subject is travelling at running speed or above you'll probably find yourself needing to use speeds above

1/1000sec, but this can cause a problem. As your shutter speeds get shorter, less light is reaching the sensor so you'll need to use a wider aperture to compensate. There may come a point where you run out of apertures and there just isn't enough light for you to use the shutter speed that you want. At this point you'll need to raise the ISO to a level that will give you the settings that you need to use.

With fast-moving subjects it's also quite risky using wide apertures because the shallow depth of field that results runs the risk of your subject drifting out of the zone of focus just as you press the shutter.

THE SLOW SHUTTER SPEED APPROACH

Freezing fast-moving subjects works some of the time but it isn't always the best way to go. It can just make your subject appear stationary. A better plan can often be to use a slower shutter speed to introduce some deliberate, controlled blur, which will better convey the sense of motion. There are several ways to approach this. If you keep the camera still and allow the subject to move through the frame, they record as a blurred streak. How blurred will depend on the shutter speed you use and the speed of the motion, so you'll need to experiment. Start with something like 1/30sec and work from there.

More often than not though, it's more fruitful to use the panning technique, which involves tracking the motion of the subject with the camera, keeping them at roughly the same place in the frame. With this method the subject will stay relatively sharp but you'll get horizontal streaking in the background which conveys that sense of speed beautifully.

PANNING CONVEYS MOTION WELL. SELECT A SLOWISH SHUTTER SPEED (1/15SEC IN THIS CASE) THEN MOVE THE CAMERA LATERALLY DURING THE EXPOSURE, TO BLUR THE BACKGROUND.

FAST SHUTTER SPEEDS CAN BE USED TO FREEZE FAST ACTION — IDEAL FOR WHEN YOU WANT TO CAPTURE A FLEETING MOMENT. 1/250SEC WAS USED HERE.

OFF-CAMERA FLASH

CREATE STUDIO-STYLE IMAGES ON LOCATION WITH YOUR FLASHGUN

One of the biggest revolutions in photography over the past couple of years has been ability to unshackle your flashgun from the confines of your camera's hotshoe and triggering it remotely from another position.

Referred to either as off-camera flash or strobist photography, it allows light to be emitted off-centre, producing a much more sculptured and professional-looking lighting effect, rather than just illuminating your subject face-on, which can produce relatively flat looking images in most cases.

Even by using a single flashgun off-camera, it's possible to achieve some really dramatic lighting effects, while extra flashguns and diffusers can all be added to the creative mix. While there's nothing stopping you from using off-camera flash at home just like you would studio lights, they really come into their own out on location thanks to their size and battery power, allowing you to control the lighting anywhere you go, so you can get creative striking studio-style lighting out on location.

Strobist photography is great fun, and it's even easier than you think to get started. Let's see what you need... your camera and flash set-up may include everything you need already.

TRIGGERING YOUR FLASHGUN REMOTELY

While it's possible to connect your flashgun directly to your camera via a dedicated sync lead, it's not the most refined solution. Instead, it's possible to trigger your flashgun wirelessly, and the beauty is, if you've got a flashgun, you can probably do it already without the need to invest in extra kit.

This is because quite a lot of cameras (predominantly DSLRs and system cameras) use their built-in flash to wirelessly trigger the remotely positioned flashgun, so when the shutter's fired the camera transmits an infrared signal to your flashgun firing it automatically. So sophisticated are these systems that they even allow Flash TTL metering to ensure the shots are exposed correctly.

While lower-end DSLRs and system cameras may not feature wireless flash control, most mid-price models and up will allow you to trigger a flash remotely with your built-in flash. This will allow you to control a set of flashguns, including whether you want to have the exposure of the remote flashgun controlled through TTL or manually (which then lets you remotely set the power output of the flashgun or 'guns), as well as any exposure compensation you want to dial in. If you're worried about the built-in flash having an effect on your image, you can control it so it will trigger the flashgun but not emit light onto your subject. That said, you might want to add a bit of fill light from your on-camera flash.

While an affordable route into off-camera flash control, triggering your flashgun via the built-in flash does have a couple of downsides. First you'll need a direct line-of-sight between camera and flashgun, while the working distance of around 10m (even less outside) can be limiting.

USING A SINGLE FLASH POSITIONED TO THE RIGHT OF THE MODEL HAS ACHIEVED A MUCH MORE PROFESSIONAL LOOKING RESULT.

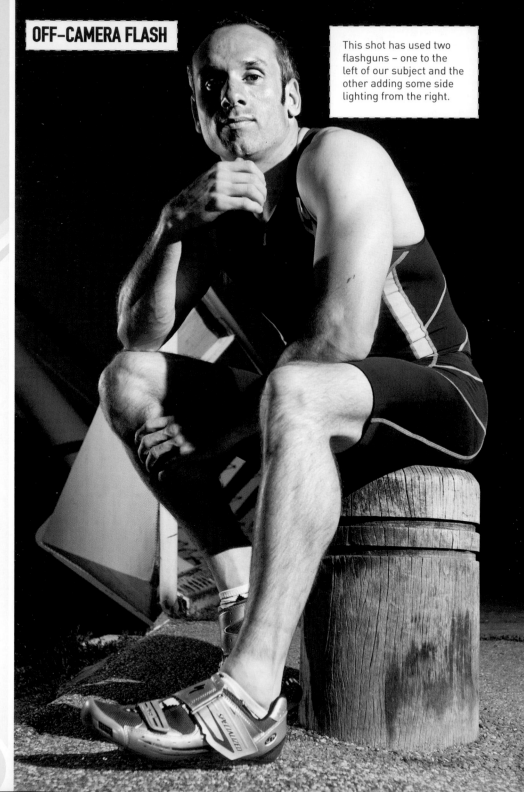

OFF-CAMERA FLASH

This shot has used two flashguns – one to the left of our subject and the other adding some side lighting from the right.

REMOTE TRIGGERS

For many photographers who want to get into wireless flash photography seriously, then the alternative is radio triggers. Offering a much better range than your built-in flashgun's infrared trigger, line-of-sight is no longer an issue, allowing flashguns to be positioned out of view of your camera for some really interesting lighting set-ups.

Radio triggers come in pairs – a transmitter attaching to your camera's PC sync socket and/or hotshoe and a receiver that connects to the flashgun via the hotshoe and/or PC sync socket. Some systems are sold as Transceiver sets, where both units can act as either a transmitter or receiver for added flexibility and other features.

While some systems offer TTL control, most will require you to set the flash power manually. This can sound quite daunting, but it's easy to experiment and review images on the back of your camera's rear screen, while once you've dialled in the correct power for the flash, you'll be provided with a consistent exposure throughout the shoot.

CHAPTER TWO

CHOOSING AND USING YOUR KIT≫

ESSENTIAL GEAR

BEFORE YOU EVEN BEGIN TAKING PICTURES, ENSURE YOU HAVE THE GEAR THAT SUITS YOUR PHOTOGRAPHY BEST. HERE IS WHAT YOU NEED TO CONSIDER

THE CAMERA

You don't need a complex or expensive camera to take a basic photograph, but as your ambitions and aspirations grow, you'll probably want to upgrade your gear too.

For any enthusiast photographer, image quality is probably going to be near the top of the wants list and, in general, the bigger the physical dimensions of the sensor the better the image quality will be.

The problem is that bigger sensors need bigger cameras to house them, and larger lenses to cover them, so a compromise must be made between image quality and portability. Before buying a camera you need to decide where on that quality/portability scale your own needs lie.

IMAGE QUALITY

Within a given sensor size and type, variations in image quality are determined largely by the resolution, in megapixels, and the quality of the processor.

While more megapixels can theoretically provide more fine detail and the ability to make bigger enlargements of your pictures, the downside is that the pixels will be smaller, so their light-gathering abilities will not be as good. The result is that the images will probably be noisier in low light.

ESSENTIAL GEAR

HIGHER IMAGE QUALITY
LESS PORTABLE

FULL FRAME DSLR

APS-C DSLR/ CSC

MICRO FOUR THIRDS CSC

1 CSC

BRIDGE CAMERA

COMPACT CAMERA

LOWER IMAGE QUALITY
MORE PORTABLE

So this calls for another decision: what's more important, fine detail at low ISOs, or low noise at high ISOs? If you shoot landscapes or in the studio it will almost certainly be the former, but if street photography or sports is more your thing then you'll probably find the latter more useful.

Even in cameras with sensors of the same size and pixel count the image quality can vary because some are better at processing that information and turning the light map captured by the sensor into what we would call a photograph. The processor is not only central to how the image looks, it also governs how quickly it is created and saved to the card, as well as other things like on-board filter effects and special features

A camera that's fast to start up, focus and shoot, and which has a fast frame rate, will be more useful to an action photographer than a landscape photographer.

While an interchangeable-lens camera is useful for most types of photography and greatly expands the creative possibilities, many street photographers prefer more discreet cameras with smaller form factors and fixed standard or wideangle lenses, although the emergence of the compact system camera has provided yet another alternative.

Wildlife and sports photographers who can't get close to their subjects will appreciate the ability to attach big telephoto lenses, but for those want neither the expense or the bulk of such lenses, bridge cameras offer very long built-in zooms in a small, lightweight body – though the performance and image quality is not in the same league as a digital SLR.

In short, there's a place for every type of camera, and choosing the right one is, first, a matter of working out what you'll be using it for, what level of image quality you require and how much weight you want to carry.

RECOMMENDED ACCESSORIES

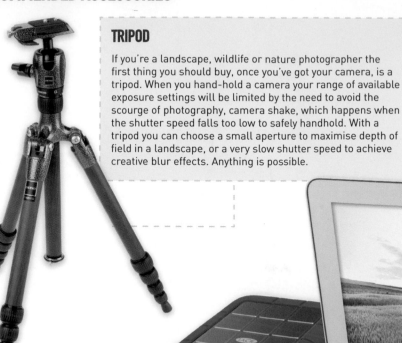

TRIPOD

If you're a landscape, wildlife or nature photographer the first thing you should buy, once you've got your camera, is a tripod. When you hand-hold a camera your range of available exposure settings will be limited by the need to avoid the scourge of photography, camera shake, which happens when the shutter speed falls too low to safely handhold. With a tripod you can choose a small aperture to maximise depth of field in a landscape, or a very slow shutter speed to achieve creative blur effects. Anything is possible.

HARD DRIVE

It's vital you archive your photos for safe keeping if you don't want to risk losing them. Whether you go for a mains or portable option you can get 1 terrabyte of storage for a reasonable price.

FLASHGUN

Flashguns have a variety of uses, not just for low light shooting. In bright sun they can fill in shadows, and the latest wireless technology makes it easier than ever to use them as a main light source instead of studio lighting. Look for models with bounce heads and wireless functionality.

COMPUTER

You may already have a powerful desktop PC but there's a lot to be said for the portability of a laptop. Beware of netbooks that aren't powerful enough for photo processing.

ND GRAD FILTERS

Landscape photographers should have these high on the shopping list. Tinted on one half and clear on the other they reduce the sky's brightness level to match that of the ground, so that the sensor can record detail in both. They come in different strengths and can be combined.

MONOPAD

Using big, heavy lenses with moving subjects poses a conundrum. You need something to keep the camera steady but a tripod restricts the ability to move and reposition the camera quickly. The monopod offers a great solution, by taking the weight of your lens, but being just one leg its easy to quickly reposition the camera whenever you need to. While you can't shoot at exposures of several seconds using a monopod exposures of around 1/2 sec are possible if you're careful.

CAMERA BAG

A decent bag that's big enough to house your key gear and keep it protected from knocks and the elements is an essential purchase. Choose from backpacks, shoulder and messenger bags and hard cases, depending on your preference. Most have adjustable compartments that can be adapted to any configuration.

ACCESSORIES

THERE ARE MANY ACCESSORIES AVAILABLE FOR YOUR DSLR THAT CAN ENHANCE YOUR PICTURE-TAKING

TRIPOD

As already stated, a tripod is possibly the most useful accessory you can own, and if you're into landscapes it's an essential item. Tripods enable you to shoot at slow shutter speeds where otherwise you'd get camera shake. This makes them great for when you want to use very small apertures for maximum depth of field as well as night and low light photography, shooting indoors, shooting panoramas, and also for posed portraits, since it will enable you to communicate more easily with your model without having the camera obscuring your face.

Tripods come in all sizes and prices. A sturdy one is best, but if you're going to have to carry it you may prefer to sacrifice some stability for portability. Carbon fibre tripods offer the best balance between weight and stability, but cost more.

FLASHGUN

The flash that is built into most cameras is adequate for emergencies but suffers from several major limitations. Firstly it's small and not very powerful; secondly it's so close to the lens that its light quality is poor and, in dim light, red-eye is a major risk. A separate flashgun will not only give you more power, but also, with the higher-spec guns, the ability to bounce the light off walls or ceilings to diffuse it (for a more natural look) or use it off camera altogether for more creative lighting effects. Some flashguns offer more advanced features such as the ability to adjust the output for more subtle effects, or be fired remotely, or produce strobe bursts for multiple flash images on the same frame.

REMOTE RELEASE

A remote release enables you to fire the camera's shutter without touching the camera itself. This reduces the risk of camera shake and helps produce sharper images. With a wireless release you don't have to be next to the camera to trigger it, making it ideal for nature and wildlife for example, when you can retreat to where you won't be seen by your subject.

POLARISER

AFTER

BEFORE

FILTERS

Filters screw on the front of your lens, and there are many types available, all with specific functions.

• UV / skylight filter: This filter is virtually clear and is designed to reduce haze and ultraviolet light, which can cause a bluish cast on your pictures. It's also often used to protect the front element of your lens from possible damage.

• Polariser: One of the most useful filters, it reduces reflections on water, glass etc and makes colours brighter and more saturated. Blue skies will be bluer, grass greener.

• Neutral Density (ND): These reduce the light entering the lens but don't affect the colour. These are ideal for when you want to use slow shutter speeds for creative effects but the light is too bright for you to do so. A graduated ND filter is grey on the top half, clear at the bottom, and is useful for darkening the sky without affecting the foreground. An essential for bringing out sky detail in landscape photography.

ND FILTER

BAGS AND HOLDALLS

As you start to accumulate extra lenses and accessories, you'll need a dedicated bag to keep them in. There are many varieties, sizes and styles to choose from. A shoulder bag gives you quick access to your gear when you need it, but if it's heavy it can give you backache after a while. A backpack distributes the weight more comfortably but you have to take it off to get to your gear, which is not always convenient.

CHOOSING A TRIPOD HEAD

TRIPODS DON'T HAVE TO COME AS A MATCHING HEAD AND LEG OUTFIT, SO IF YOUR HEAD ISN'T QUITE UP TO THE TASK THEN PERHAPS YOU NEED AN UPGRADE. HERE ARE A FEW DIFFERENT OPTIONS FOR A VARIETY OF PHOTOGRAPHY STYLES

HEAD STYLE

When buying a tripod head it pays to actually use it before purchase so you can be sure it's the right one for you. If you're unsure which type is most suitable for your needs have a play with each to help come to a decision.

Almost every photographer needs a tripod – it's just one of those accessories everyone can find a use for. Let's assume you've chosen a tripod that meets all of your needs and budget, and now you need to pick a tripod head that fits the same criteria. The great thing is that you don't have to loyally stick to the same manufacturer – you can mix and match heads and legs to create the perfect combination for you. Choosing the best head for your style of photography is very important, but it mostly comes down to personal taste and budget. There are three main types of tripod head to choose from for photography, although there are numerous options within these groups and specialist heads too. The first, and most common type is the 3-way head. These can be moved and adjusted using three handles or knobs. They're generally slower to use than a ball head, but are sometimes effective when it comes to achieving a level composition.

Ball heads use a much simpler design than the 3-way, in that they're like a ball and socket joint. This makes them quick and easy to use because you loosen the ball, reposition the camera and then tighten up once the shot has been composed. They're great for composing quickly, but where they fall down is with long heavy lenses. If you're a motorsport or wildlife photographer there's a much better option available for you. Gimbal heads are both specialist and expensive compared to the previous types of head. However, if you often shoot with a long telephoto lens this type of head can be invaluable. Gimbal heads are designed to balance the camera and lens at their centre of gravity,

so they remain stable when moved quickly and smoothly without the tripod having to be set to a locked position. This makes the gimbal perfect for subjects where the lens must be kept steady, during up, down and panning movements.

So there are the three main head types, but within these groups there are numerous

options so there are a few considerations you have to make. Think about the overall weight of the head and its maximum load. Can it take your camera and lenses? Are the knobs and handles easy to operate? How smooth is the overall operation of the head and can it be used in landscape and portrait format?

LEG COMPATIBILITY

When you buy a good quality tripod you most often have to buy a head separately. This doesn't mean you have to loyally stick to a single brand – you can mix and match.

SIZE & WEIGHT

The overall size and weight of the head is an important consideration, as you don't want something too big and heavy that has to be carried around when shooting landscapes. And if you shoot mostly in the studio you don't want something too small and light.

LENS TYPES

STANDARD ZOOM

LOOKING FOR A NEW LENS? WHICH ONE WILL ALLOW YOU TO GET THE SHOTS YOU WANT?

18-35mm 1:1.8 DC Ø72

SIGMA

35 28 24 20 18

0.71 2 ∞ FEET M

AAA10123

Most DSLRs and CSCs are bundled with a standard zoom, offering a versatile lens for general photography, covering moderate wideangle to short telephoto. This makes them ideal general-purpose lenses, suitable for the majority of the kind of shots that most people take regularly, from scenic views to portraits.

These kit lenses do a fairly remarkable job considering that they're designed to be as cheap as possible to make, so that they add as little as possible to the cost of buying a new camera. The image quality of these lenses is more than adequate for general snaps but if you aspire to produce images of the highest technical

standard, then you're much better off forsaking the kit lens in favour of a premium alternative. They'll probably be a lot bigger and heavier but they'll have wider maximum apertures and far superior edge-to-edge resolution.

WIDEANGLE ZOOM

Wideangle lenses make subjects appear further away, so they are useful when you can't stand back far enough to get everything you want in shot – such as when photographing a large building, an expansive view or large group shot. But they also produce an apparent perspective distortion in which subjects close to the camera can appear disproportionately larger than those further away – an effect that can be used by the photographer in all sorts of creative ways. They also give the illusion of placing the viewer in the thick of the action, which makes them popular with reportage and street photographers.

Although wideangles are available in various fixed focal lengths, a good wideangle zoom, covering a range of focal lengths, is often the smarter bet. Optically the best ones are on a par with many premium primes; they are often hardly any bigger and may even cost less.

TELEPHOTO ZOOM

Telephoto lenses have a narrower field of view than wider optics, enabling you to crop in on details and magnify more distant subjects. They're perfect for photographing things that you can't get physically close to (at least, not safely) such as elusive wildlife subjects and many sports.

Telephoto lenses imbue your images with certain aesthetic traits, such as shallower depth of field, and the sense of compressing distance so that elements further away in your scene seem right on top of closer ones.

Exotic and expensive prime telephoto lenses are the choice of pros, but zooms offer the advantage of allowing you to zoom in or out to get the exact framing you want, which is especially useful given that in many of the situations in which you'd use one you may not be able to freely move around. They can be considerably cheaper too.

SUPERZOOM

Many people are drawn to the idea of a single lens that covers every focal range from 18mm wideangle to 200mm telephoto and beyond. Such an optic would avoid the need to ever change the lens, and of course you'd never get dust on your sensor when swapping lenses.

There are trade-offs with such lenses. In general, the longer the range, the more the optical quality tends to suffer, with lower contrast, poorer edge sharpness and greater distortion.

The maximum apertures are pretty small too (as low as f/6.3 at the tele end) so you may have to raise the ISO more often to shoot handheld.

However, you may find these to be sacrifices worth making, with these optics being fine for users who want reasonably good pictures that won't be printed too big or studied with a magnifying glass, while the size also makes them tempting for those who travel a lot.

FAST PRIME

OLYMPUS   75 mm   1:1.8   MSC

0.8m/2.6ft - ∞

Zoom lenses are almost ubiquitous now but fixed focal length, or "prime", lenses continue to be popular because they offer several advantages. Since they only have to convey a single field of view, as opposed to having to offer a variable range, the optical performance is generally superior.

They tend to be smaller too, and as an extra bonus have wider maximum apertures. If the field of view they offer is the one that you want, and you can fine-tune your cropping simply by moving your position, then they have a lot to offer.

Primes cover the full spectrum of focal lengths from extreme wide to ultra telephoto, but the most useful for general photography are those in the 24mm to 85mm range. They needn't cost the earth either.

MACRO

If you want to shoot close-ups, then you need a macro lens. To be a true macro lens it must enable you to reproduce your subject at 1:1 lifesize on your sensor, but many lenses (particularly zooms) carry the word "macro" in their title that only offer around a quarter lifesize (1:4). Whilst still useful for general shooting, they're no good for really close-up work.

Macro lenses can also be used for general photography, as they can focus from infinity right down to 1:1 on a single rotation of the focus ring. Most true macro lenses are prime optics, with the most common focal lengths being around 50mm and 100mm, though there are also a few around the 200mm range. The advantage of the more telephoto macros is that you can shoot from further away, so if you're photographing shy subjects such as butterflies you don't have to be so close to them, and you don't cast a shadow.

LENS ACCESSORIES

THERE'S A VARIETY OF ADD-ONS YOU CAN BUY TO MODIFY YOUR LENS' BEHAVIOUR OR SPECIFICATION

There are many accessories that have been developed to alter the characteristics of your lens, typically to increase focal length or enable macro shooting, and as they're available from several manufacturers the choice usually caters for all budgets.

So rather than having to invest in additional lenses, you can adapt an existing optic to mimic the characteristics of another lens. Not only is it a more affordable solution, but they will usually also weigh far less and be less of a burden to carry around.

Then there are filters and lens hoods, which largely don't enable any particular effect but simply allow the photographer to control the light entering the lens. And should you ever feel limited by the lenses within your own system you can always use an adaptor to mount optics developed for others. When looked at as a whole, therefore, the lens accessory market is an exciting world of photographic possibilities; and, since many accessories can be used in combination with one another, what's achievable is only limited by the user's creativity.

LENS CONVERTERS

Lens converters are an inexpensive way to change the focal length of a lens. They screw into the filter thread of an existing optic, and offer a fisheye, wideangle or telephoto view. As they can be mounted onto a variety of lenses they are classified by magnification factor rather than a focal length; this must be multiplied by your lens focal length to give the combined effective focal length. So, a 0.70x wideangle converter turns a 50mm optic into one with an effective 35mm length. Cheaper converters are likely to have poor control over chromatic aberrations and will almost certainly degrade image quality, but superior options are also available.

66

TELECONVERTERS

Teleconverters sit between a camera body and lens, and their purpose is to increase the latter's effective focal length. With an optical arrangement within their construction, they allow light which would otherwise exit the lens and come to focus on the sensor to continue travelling through the system, thus increasing the effective focal length of the set-up.

They are most commonly found in 1.4x and 2x varieties, figures which relate to their multiplication factor against a lens's focal length. So, a 300mm f/2.8 lens used with the former will yield an effective focal length of 420mm, and with the latter will double the figure to 600mm. Other varieties such as 1.7x and 3x teleconverters also exist, although these are less popular options.

As the strength of a teleconverter increases it reduces the amount of light which passes through to the sensor, and so it decreases the maximum aperture of the optic. A 1.4x converter cuts down light transmission by one EV stop while a 2x converter cuts down two EV stops, so with the above lens this will impose respective limits of f/4 and f/5.6. Considering the shallow depth of field associated with longer focal lengths this reduction may not prove restrictive from a creative standpoint, although any increase in effective focal length also requires that shutter speed be raised to help keep the image sharp (which obviously becomes more difficult if the maximum aperture is made smaller).

Manufacturers often recommend that their own brand teleconverters be used with their lenses. While not all lenses are compatible with them – more affordable optics with slower maximum apertures tend not to be suited to use with a teleconverter, as the maximum aperture would decrease so much that it's not really usable. Check on your manufacturer's website to see if your lens is compatible, while third-party options are also available.

Teleconverters can affect the optical quality of the lens, while the reduction in light can make it harder for AF systems to acquire focus. That said, they're a much more affordable (and lightweight) alternative to investing in large expensive telephoto lenses.

Teleconverters will extend the working distance of your camera, while reversing rings can be a cheap way to shoot macro.

LENS ACCESSORIES

EXTENSION TUBES AND REVERSING RINGS

True macro lenses can be expensive, but a number of cheaper alternatives are also available, such as extension tubes. Unlike teleconverters, tubes have no glass elements, but simply extend the distance between lens and camera body. This means you can go past the minimum focusing distance determined by the lens, effectively magnifying your subject.

Because they contain no additional optics, tubes don't affect the optical quality of a lens. They're usually supplied as a set of three which can be used either on their own or in combination with one another. Those that have contacts provide support for both metering and autofocus, though for static subjects it may be easier to switch to manual focus for greater precision.

With some extension tubes, such as those with no electronic contacts, you may also need to meter differently from the way in which you are used to, as the connection between the camera and lens which ordinarily facilitates aperture control will be broken.

An alternative to extension tubes is reversing rings. These simply allow a lens to be reverse-mounted onto a camera, and with the contacts facing outwards the camera loses communication with the lens. This set-up has a fixed working distance, while lenses without aperture rings will also need to be used wide open. This all may sound like too much trouble, but this can easily and cheaply create a high-magnification set up, and with modern live view systems it shouldn't be too difficult to judge correct exposure and focus either.

Extension tubes and close-up lenses allow close-up photography without the need for a dedicated macro lens. Shown here: extension tubes from Kenko (back left) and SRB Griturn (rear right) and close-up lenses (sometimes referred to as filters) from Hoya and B+W.

FILTERS

Filters are one of the most obvious lens accessories, and have been used for decades for tonal and colour control. The most common are ultraviolet (UV) filters, which many photographers keep permanently on their lenses for protection, and polarisers which are useful for darkening skies and minimising reflections. Neutral density (ND) filters, both graduated and non-graduated, are also widely used to control exposure. Many other types of filters exist, but the rise of digital photography has caused their popularity to drop. Polarisers and ND filters remain the only two filters whose effects are required while shooting, which explains why they have remained the most popular choices.

MOUNT ADAPTORS

Most people will only tend to use lenses developed specifically for their camera system, although there are many reasons why you may want to use a lens manufactured with a different mount.

Perhaps the lens you wish to use isn't available in your system's mount, or you may have at some point switched systems without trading in all of your glass. Another possibility is that you made the transition from a manufacturer's analogue system to its digital one and, again, kept your lenses in the hope that you could one day get some use out of them. Whatever the reason, the likelihood is that an adaptor exists for the task.

Manufacturers such as SRB-Photon, Novoflex and Voigtländer all specialize in producing adaptors that can mount older optics from a variety of systems onto newer bodies, while a quick search online reveals an endless assortment of unbranded adaptors which can be picked up for next to nothing.

There are a few points to bear in mind when using adaptors with other optics. With no connection between the camera and lens, similar limitations occur as with extension tubes without contacts – namely that more automated control over aperture isn't possible. Metering, therefore, must occur at the aperture you plan to use for your exposure. You may also need to adjust your camera's settings so that it will work with unrecognised lenses, and as many older lenses predate autofocus they will also need to be manually focused.

MOUNT ADAPTORS ALLOW YOU TO USE DIFFERENT FIT LENSES ON YOUR CAMERA.

CHAPTER THREE
UNDERSTANDING YOUR CAMERA »

Camera Controls

CAMERA CONTROLS

GETTING YOUR CAMERA OFF THE AUTO-EVERYTHING SETTINGS IS THE FIRST STEP TO TAKING CREATIVE CONTROL OF YOUR IMAGES. HERE ARE A FEW KEY ONES

Shooting in Raw gives you a lot more options at the processing stage, including the ability to change the white balance, adjust the exposure, recover highlight and shadow detail and much more.

USE RAW

If you have the option to shoot raw files on your camera you should use it, even if you also use the more convenient jpeg format. Although Raw files take up more space on your card and are more of a hassle to process on your PC, they offer such compelling advantages that for anyone aspiring to produce the highest quality images

possible, it's difficult to justify not shooting in raw. While jpegs are fine for snaps, they are essentially raw files that have been processed by the camera, and large amounts of the recorded data will have been discarded, in order to reduce the file size. If it turns out you got things wrong you're limited in what you can do to fix it.

With raw files all the captured data is kept, and the camera leaves you to decide what the image should look like later. The advantages of this are that you get more creative control, the image quality will be higher and, crucially, you can change the white balance and even adjust the exposure by a couple of stops at the processing stage if you got it wrong when you shot it.

Image quality deteriorates as the ISO is raised, so use the lowest ISO you can for the conditions you're shooting in. For portraits in good light (left), ISO 100 was fine, but the picture of the steam train engineer stoking his engine (right) was taken in near total darkness and required the highest setting available.

ISO 100

ISO 12800

SHOOTING IN BOTH RAW AND JPEG MAY TAKE UP MORE SPACE ON YOUR MEDIA CARD BUT IT GIVES YOU BOTH THE CONVENIENCE OF JPEG AND THE SECURITY OF A RAW FILE IF YOU NEED IT.

TAKE CONTROL OF YOUR ISO

The ISO setting controls the sensitivity of your camera's sensor. The more sensitive it is the less light it needs to record an exposure, which is great when there isn't enough ambient light to give you the shutter speed or aperture you want to use – but there is a downside.

As you raise the ISO the image quality is detrimentally affected. With the better cameras this isn't really noticeable at ISO's up to around 400, but once you get over 1000 you'll be able to see an increase in noise

– tiny speckles, sometimes of coloured dots, that cover your picture. They're most visible in shadows, and areas of uniform tone. The higher your ISO, the more visible that noise becomes. Noise can not only be distracting but has the effect of breaking up the fine detail in the image. Most cameras employ two kinds of noise-reduction system: one for high ISOs and the other for the noise that occurs with long exposures of over a second. While the latter works quite well, high ISO noise reduction works by

attempting to blur the noise so that it's less visible, but in doing so it also reduces the sharpness of your image. There are times when you have no alternative but to use a higher ISO, such as when shooting handheld in low light, or when photographing moving subjects in light that isn't bright enough to allow for a fast shutter speed.

The rule of thumb is to use the lowest ISO setting that will give you the exposure settings that you need in order to get your shot.

73

CAMERA CONTROLS

MANUAL WHITE BALANCE

AUTO WHITE BALANCE

WHEN THE LIGHT HAS AN APPEALING COLOUR, SUCH AS AT SUNSET, THE CAMERA WILL ATTEMPT TO REMOVE SOME OF THE COLOUR IF LEFT IN THE AUTO WHITE BALANCE MODE. SWITCH TO MANUAL OR SHOOT IN RAW SO YOU CAN CORRECT THE COLOUR LATER.

WATCH YOUR WHITE BALANCE

Light comes in many colours but our eyes adjust for it automatically so we seldom notice. Cameras, however, do, and are well aware that tungsten light, for example, is much more orange than daylight, and the auto white balance corrects for that. But in doing so it can sometimes destroy the atmosphere in a scene, especially if, for example, that atmosphere

was partially created by a particularly warm or cool light. Your camera will attempt to remove this, as it's been programmed to do.

A perfect example is a warm sunset, where the camera will try to reduce the strong yellow orange light that attracted you to photograph it in the first place. It's generally better to use the white balance presets on

the camera, such as sunny, cloudy, tungsten etc., rather than letting the camera try to guess. This especially is the case with artificial light shots.

Better still, take a reading of the light temperature and set this exactly. Of course, if you shoot in raw this is less important as you can always change it later.

This image illustrates the difference in colour between daylight and artificial light. Daylight is more blue, tungsten more orange. If you're shooting indoors in artificial light be sure to set the white balance to the correct setting, or take a custom white balance reading from the scene for the most accurate results.

This snow-scene is a classic example of how the camera's meter can go wrong when faced with mainly light or dark subjects.

AUTO EXPOSURE

TAKE CARE WITH EXPOSURE

Your camera's exposure meter works on the assumption that most scenes comprise a roughly equal proportion of light and dark areas, so setting an exposure somewhere in the middle will produce a good image. But this doesn't work if your scene is predominantly light, such as a snow scene, or mostly dark like a night scene. With light scenes the camera will try to darken them and with dark ones it will try to lighten them, resulting in either under- or over-exposure. Clearly the meter needs to be kept an eye on, and exposure compensation used when it gets things wrong.

For creative photographers correct exposure is subjective. It's not about averages, it's about exposing for specific areas of the scene to get a certain result. Expose for the highlights, for example, and it will record as a mid-tone in a sea of black.

If you want white areas to stay white in your final image, you may need to set the exposure compensation dial to +1 or +2 stops, depending on the situation.

+1.3 STOP EXPOSURE COMPENSATION

Using +1.3 stops of exposure compensation has made the snow white again, as it should be.

SHOOTING MODES

YOUR CAMERA OFFERS A BEWILDERING CHOICE OF EXPOSURE MODES, BUT WHAT DO THEY ALL DO?

All DSLRs, Compact System Cameras and many of the more advanced compacts offer a selection of modes which give you varying degrees of control over the exposure, and how it is arrived at. Many cameras feature mode dials like the one shown here. If not then they'll be selectable via a top plate LCD, or the rear display screen. The specific aperture or shutter speed you choose, in tandem with the ISO

setting, can have a profound effect on what the final picture looks like. If you want to get creative with your image making, rather than just taking snaps in which the camera has made all the decisions, then you need to steer clear of the full auto and scene modes and get to grips with some of the other exposure modes on offer. Here's a run-down of what they do, and when to use them.

> MOST CAMERAS PROVIDE A DIAL TO SELECT EXPOSURE MODES, BUT WITH SOME IT'S DONE VIA A TOP LCD OR THE REAR SCREEN.

EXPOSURE MODES EXPLAINED

"GREEN" AUTO

In this mode the camera takes full control of the exposure, metering, white balance, ISO, focusing, flash and drive modes. Most full auto modes are now "intelligent" in that they use scene recognition to identify the type of subject and thus switch to the appropriate scene mode.

SHUTTER PRIORITY

Use this mode to take control of the shutter speed. Set a high speed to freeze movement or a slower one to add creative blur, and the camera will set the corresponding aperture to provide the correct exposure. If using slow speeds you'll need a support to avoid camera shake.

MANUAL MODE

In manual mode you have to set both aperture and shutter speed to get a correct exposure. It's ideal when you need shot-to-shot consistency, such as for stitching panoramas, where auto would be influenced by elements in the scene. It's also the mode to use with studio flash.

FILTER EFFECTS

These produce effects that would require time and skill to do in Photoshop. Cross processing, tilt/shift, grainy b&w and high/low key are some of the most popular. Shoot Raw if you can so you get a "straight" shot too, in case you don't like the result from the filter.

PROGRAM

Program mode also controls everything for you but allows some user input. You can alter the aperture/shutter speed combination, choose to use flash or not, and select ISO and white balance manually. This is a good place to start for beginners who want to take control gradually.

APERTURE PRIORITY

Use this mode if you want to take charge of the depth of field in an image, and let the camera take care of the shutter speed. The smaller your aperture the more of the scene comes into focus, but still keep an eye on the shutter speed to ensure it doesn't become too slow to handhold.

SCENE MODES

Scene modes are full auto modes, but by telling the camera what you're photographing it's able to choose settings more likely to get you a good result – e.g. fast speeds for action, wide apertures for portraits. They may be marked on the dial or found in the menu (or both).

OTHER MODES

 A dedicated movie mode gives access to manual controls when shooting video.

Custom Modes allow you to save specific shooting parameters to a dial setting, for quick access when needed.

 Tutorial-based modes offering advice and tips.

DRIVE MODES

Drive Modes

DRIVE MODES CONTROL HOW QUICKLY YOU CAN TAKE PHOTOS

Drive modes are a important setting on your camera, as they control whether you take single or multiple shots when the shutter button is fully depressed. Not only that, but they can also be used to delay the shutter being fired after you've fired the shutter button.

The drive mode you choose will depend a lot on the subject you're taking – a sports shot, for instance, where you want to ensure you capture the action will require a series of multiple shots in quick succession; whereas a still-life or portrait shot won't require that same split-second accuracy, so a different drive mode is required. Below are the four main drive modes found on a camera.

> SELECTING THE CORRECT DRIVE MODE MAKES A MASSIVE DIFFERENCE TO HOW YOU SHOOT.

DRIVE MODES EXPLAINED

SINGLE

Your camera's single drive mode is your camera's default shooting mode and, for most of us, the drive mode you'll use the most as it's perfect for a range of shooting situations, from portraits to landscapes.

As the name suggests, when you press the shutter button, a single shot is taken, regardless of how long you hold the shutter button down for. If you want to take another shot, you'll need to release it and press the shutter button down again.

CONTINUOUS

This is the best mode for when you're shooting action because it will allow you to press and hold the shutter button down and fire off a series of shots in a non-stop burst to ensure you get the winning shot.

The rate at which the camera fires continuously depends on the model, ranging from 2.5fps (frames per second) to 12fps, while some models are able to sustain longer bursts than others. You'll find that the camera will stop shooting as it tries to process all that data.

SELF-TIMER

The self-timer mode isn't just ideal for getting yourself in the frame, as it comes in handy for other situations too.

If you're taking a shot with the camera on a tripod for instance, use the self-timer, as even though the camera is supported, pressing the shutter button can induce movement. In self-timer mode though, any slight movement will have subsided by the time the shutter is triggered. Most cameras have two-second and 10-second delays, some even more.

QUIET MODES

Quiet mode (also known as silent) is a relatively new mode that's found its way on to DSLRs over the past couple of years, so some models may not feature it.

The noise of the shutter can be quite loud, so to reduce this the mirror is not lowered until the shutter button is released, allowing you to choose when the camera releases the mirror. As well as this, the beep sound your camera makes when focus is acquired is disabled.

FLASH

FROM ILLUMINATING YOUR SUBJECT TO CREATIVE SHOTS, FLASH CAN BE INCREDIBLY POWERFUL

Most cameras either feature a built-in flash or one that attaches to the camera.

Even though these little flashes aren't that powerful, they can still be very useful, from simply illuminating your subject in a poorly lit scene to achieving creative effects.

Trouble is, it can seem a bit confusing if you haven't used flash that much before, especially if your camera features an array of flash modes to choose from.

Here we'll explain everything you need to know about your basic flash settings on your camera, from simple Auto modes through to advanced controls that allow you to balance the flash with the scene for creative shots.

> HAVING A GOOD UNDERSTANDING OF HOW YOUR FLASH WORKS IS VITAL IF YOU'D LIKE TO CREATE STRIKING PHOTOGRAPHS.

FLASH MODES EXPLAINED

AUTO

If you're going to be shooting in one of your camera's Auto shooting modes (one of the Scene modes for instance), the camera will only fire the flash when the lighting drops below a certain level. Fine for snaps, but it won't deliver the best balanced, professional-looking shots.

REDEYE

A camera's redeye flash mode will send out a pre-flash before the shutter is fired and the main flash is triggered. The pronounced delay between the two flashes can lead to subjects not knowing when to pose/smile, resulting in unflattering images.

FILL-IN

Fill-in is the default mode on most cameras and is really versatile. If your subject is in shade, adding a touch of fill-in flash will lighten them nicely thanks to your camera's TTL flash metering, while the background will be correctly exposed producing a well-balanced shot.

81

FLASH

SLOW-SYNC FLASH

While your flash can illuminate your subject without any problems, shooting in poorly lit conditions will often mean the background is underexposed. This is because most DSLRs have a default shutter speed of 1/60sec when shooting with flash so you can still handhold the camera.

By selecting your camera's slow-sync flash mode, you're letting the camera know that you want a more balanced exposure, so the camera will know to expose for the ambient scene as well – even if that means dropping the shutter speed down dramatically in order to do so. If that's the case, you'll need to use a tripod to avoid any camera shake.

REAR CURTAIN SLOW-SYNC FLASH

Your camera, by default, is designed to fire the flash (on-camera or off) at the beginning of the exposure. This is fine for most shooting conditions, but if you want to extend the exposure to introduce movement into the shot, it can become an issue. Subjects can look like they're moving backwards as the flash has captured them at the start of the exposure, with the ambient exposure trailing forward. To avoid this, cameras feature a rear curtain slow-sync mode (also known as second curtain), which fires the flash at the end of the exposure. A bit more anticipation is required, but it produces a much more pleasing result.

CHAPTER FOUR
LANDSCAPES »

6 STEPS TO BETTER LANDSCAPES

1 LOOK FOR LEAD-IN LINES

Lead-in lines are a very clever visual device that can be used to draw the viewers' eye through the scene and give your images a greater sense of depth. For landscape photography there are a range of scenic elements that can be used as lead-in lines including hedgerows, walls, fences, rivers, streams, paths and roads.

To incorporate them successfully into your landscape shots the best way to use lead-in lines is to have them starting at the bottom of the frame, or within the bottom-third of the shot. They should then extend into the scene as far as possible so the eye is drawn from the front of the scene and to the back of it. A common mistake is to position what should be a lead-in line across the frame – doing this creates more of a visual barrier than a lead-in line, and should be avoided at all costs.

WHY THIS SHOT WORKS

This scene doesn't really use the rule-of-thirds to tie the elements of the scene together because of the shape of the landscape. Instead it relies heavily on the path starting in the bottom left-hand corner and drawing the eye through the scene to the horizon.

2 APPLY THE RULE-OF-THIRDS

The rule-of-thirds is the backbone of the majority of compositions because of the way it creates visual balance in photos. To use this compositional device, imagine the viewfinder is split into nine equally-sized rectangles by two vertical and two horizontal lines. There are four points where these lines intersect, and it's on one of these points that the focal point of the scene should be positioned. Some cameras have guides built into the viewfinder and/or Live View on the LCD.

6 STEPS TO BETTER LANDSCAPES

3 INCLUDE FOREGROUND INTEREST

Foreground interest is another device that helps draw the eye into the scene. But rather than leading the eye through the shot like a lead-in line, foreground interest acts as a visual stepping stone into the shot. It works simply by filling empty space in the foreground that would otherwise result in a dull landscape shot. But don't just throw anything into the foreground and hope for the best. Foreground interest should be an object that's relevant to the entire scene. In this shot we've used rocks with the largest rock positioned according to the rule-of-thirds to make this the focal point of the foreground area.

As well as rocks, potential objects for use as foreground interest in a landscape could include foliage, water, mill stones or even parts of elements such as a section of wall. When composing a shot make sure there's no litter in the foreground, and no matter how tempting, don't use thistles – they never look good.

KEEP YOUR DISTANCE

When shooting foreground interest with an ultra wide-angle lens be aware of your distance from the object, so you don't hit it with your lens. Judging near distances with wide-angle lenses on the camera is very difficult!

4 SET UP YOUR TRIPOD CORRECTLY FOR LEVEL HORIZONS

Exposure times are often too slow to handhold the camera, most often due to the combination of low ISO for maximum image quality and narrow aperture for a large depth-of-field, so you'll need to use a tripod. Even if you can achieve all the necessary camera settings and still handhold the camera, it still pays to use a tripod. Why? Because it will lead to more considered compositions.

Using a tripod will slow you down, meaning you're less likely to snap away then quickly move onto the next shot with little thought.

Setting up a tripod is a simple process, essentially just extending the legs and making sure it's firmly positioned. However, there are a couple of things you can do to ensure best practice. The first sections that should be extended are the thickest ones closest to the head, then the middle sections and finally the thinnest sections if necessary. The fatter leg sections are always the most stable, so these should be used first. Only extend the centre column if the legs are fully extended. Once the tripod's set up, ensure it's firmly positioned by pushing down on two of the legs. Adjust individual leg length if necessary.

Always make sure the image stabilisation feature on your lens is turned off when using a tripod.

TRIPOD HEAD

Before setting up the tripod, frame up the shot while holding the camera. Now you have a rough idea of height and position of the camera, you need to erect the tripod so the head occupies the space where the camera was.

EXTEND THE LEGS

If the tripod doesn't need to be fully extended, extend the thicker legs first, then the middle and then the thinnest. You should only extend the centre column if the legs are fully extended because using the column reduces stability.

CHECK STABILITY

If you're setting up on bumpy ground make sure each leg is extended to match the lumps and bumps in the ground. The tripod head should be as level as possible. Once this is done, push down firmly on two tripod legs to check stability.

THREE WAYS TO ENSURE A LEVEL HORIZON

1 USE YOUR FOCUS POINTS

One of the most basic ways to achieve a level horizon is to use the focus points in the viewfinder as a guide. This method is far from perfect because you're judging with your eye, but it is much better than simply framing up and hoping for the best.

2 USE THE VIRTUAL HORIZON

All modern DSLRs have Live View, and a large number of these also have a very handy Virtual Horizon feature. It looks very similar to the altitude indicator in an aeroplane. When level you'll see a green line as above. If not it will be red and show the tilt of the camera.

3 USE A HOTSHOE SPIRIT LEVEL

One of the best ways to ensure your horizon is straight and the camera isn't tilted up or down is to use a hotshoe spirit level. These inexpensive accessories simply slide into the hotshoe when required to provide a reliable way to ensure the camera is level.

6 STEPS TO BETTER LANDSCAPES

5 EXPOSE FOR THE ENTIRE SCENE

One of the biggest problems you'll face with landscape photography is successfully exposing for all parts of the scene. Quite often the difference between the amount of light coming from the sky and the foreground is so great that when you expose for one, detail in the other is lost. To ensure we maintained detail throughout our image we shot three RAW exposures of the scene. Since the camera was attached to a tripod there was no movement between each shot taken, so they could be successfully blended together in post-processing. The first shot taken was at the camera's recommended exposure using evaluative metering.

The second was 1 stop overexposed, and the third 1 stop underexposed. Since we were shooting in aperture-priority mode at f/16, the over- and underexposure was applied using exposure compensation. To ensure clean, noise-free images of the highest quality, ISO was set to the lowest setting of 100.

OVEREXPOSED

+

UNDEREXPOSED

=

HOW TO BLEND THE EXPOSURES

With the RAW images shot you'll need to download the two or more exposures to a computer so they can be blended together. This is to ensure that detail is maintained in all areas of the scene, and the end result should look the way it did on the day.

SHADOW DETAIL

Shadow areas in photos typically contain the most noise if exposure is pushed too far in post-processing. To avoid unwanted noise it's best to expose a frame specifically for shadow areas so that exposure is perfect.

HIGHLIGHT DETAIL

The problem with blown or overexposed highlights is that once the detail is gone (pure white), there's no getting it back. The best way to maintain highlight detail is to expose one frame specifically for the highlights.

POINT OF FOCUS AND DEPTH-OF-FIELD

Get the point of focus wrong in a landscape shot and you're looking at blur, even if you're shooting at a narrow aperture like f/16. The best place to focus is one-third of the way into the scene. Combining this with the narrow aperture setting is what gives you front to back sharpness, which is a standard feature of landscape photography.

GOOD FOCUS

BAD FOCUS

6 USE MANUAL FOCUS TO CONTROL SHARPNESS

With the camera firmly attached to a tripod and the camera set to aperture-priority at a narrow setting such as f/16, there's one more important task that must be completed to ensure sharpness from the front of the scene all the way through to the back. And quite simply, it's focusing – what mode to use and where to

actually focus. The thing about focusing for landscapes is that if you get it wrong you could end up with large areas of blur. For landscape photography it's best to focus manually so you can choose the point of focus, even if it's outside of the focus point area in the camera's viewfinder. Focusing manually also means that focus will be

locked at the desired point, with no risk of changing unless you move the focusing ring on the lens.

To maximise sharpness in landscapes, you should focus one-third of the way into the scene. That's not the frame, but the distance from the front of the shot to the back.

TAKE YOUR BEST LANDSCAPE SHOTS

There are few photographic subjects that are as relaxing and enjoyable as landscapes. Now you know our six steps for better landscape shots it's time to get out into the great outdoors and try them for yourself. Whether you're in a classic location or simply the countryside close to your home, apply these steps every time to guarantee better landscape shots at any time of year, whatever the weather.

FOCUS SHOULD BE SET AT ONE-THIRD OF THE WAY INTO THE SCENE ITSELF, NOT ONE-THIRD OF THE WAY UP THE FRAME.

CITYSCAPES

London and the Thames, framed through Tower Bridge.

THE URBAN ENVIRONMENT PRESENTS PLENTY OF OPPORTUNITIES FOR GREAT IMAGES, FROM ARCHITECTURAL STUDIES TO CANDID STREET SHOTS

You don't have to head out to the countryside for good pictures. Most urban environments have plenty of photographic potential too, whether in the buildings or those who inhabit them.

ARCHITECTURE

Buildings offer a rich source of material for photography – from old churches, period cottages, and town halls dating back centuries that you find in every town and city in the country, to modern glass towers, with their sharp angles and huge potential for reflections.

VIEWPOINT

Lighting is crucial in architectural photography. But since you can't move a building it's you who must move around it, to find not only the best viewpoint but the best lighting. If those two requirements don't coincide then return at a different time of day, when the sun will be lighting a different facade.

Walk around a building to determine its most photogenic aspect. If the light is bad, work out when you'll need to return to catch it at its best. A compass and map (or Google Maps) will be useful for this.

PERSPECTIVE

Tall buildings are difficult to photograph without tilting the camera upwards, and this often causes the sides to converge inwards. To keep the sides of a building parallel you need to keep the camera level, but then you'll probably be cropping off the top of the building. There are several possible solutions.

• Move further back so that you can include the top without tilting. This may not be possible due to other buildings nearby.

• Seek a high viewpoint, such as a balcony or open window on a high floor of a building adjacent to the one you're photographing.

• Go with the distortion and correct it later in Photoshop (though this will degrade the image quality).

• If you're really serious about architecture buy a dedicated tilt and shift lens, which will enable you to get distortion-free verticals. They cost over £1,000, though.

• With some buildings you can get more dramatic shots by deliberately exaggerating the distortion. Fit a wideangle lens and point the camera directly upwards from close range. This works especially well with tall, modern buildings, where it implies a sense of height.

To keep the sides of buildings straight, keep the camera level. With tall buildings this may require shooting from further away.

Head for high viewpoints to get a good city vista, such as this one in Havana.

Don't forget to look inside buildings too, for great pictures. This was taken inside Cologne Cathedral.

SKYLINES

No record of a city would be complete without a shot of its skyline. For that you'll need to head to high ground. Do some research to find the best high viewpoints, whether they be the top of a tall building, or a hill on the outskirts of the city. For the best light you'll need to get there early in the morning, or at sunset – depending on which direction you're shooting from. Avoid the middle of the day with direct overhead light, and use a UV filter to reduce any haze, which is more prevalent at high altitudes.

STREET LIFE

There's plenty to photograph on street level without even looking at the buildings. Interesting or amusing signs, shop fronts, and situations – and of course the people. Street vendors, street performers, crowds of commuters and even fellow tourists can all be a rich source of pictures. Depending on the situation, you may either prefer to shoot candids with a telephoto lens or go in close with a wideangle. Be aware that not everyone likes being photographed – if in doubt, ask first.

DETAILS

When photographing buildings don't just look at the whole building. With churches and older period properties in particular you'll find plenty of interesting details to zoom in on, such as gargoyles and ornate stonework. With modern glass buildings, reflections can be a rich source of subject matter too. Look for juxtapositions between buildings, such as an old building framed by a modern one next to it. Telephoto lenses can be great for this. Don't forget to look inside the building too for interesting details.

TRAVEL

THE UNFAMILIAR SIGHTS AND CUSTOMS OF FOREIGN PLACES AND CULTURES HAVE LONG BEEN A GREAT INSPIRATION FOR PHOTOGRAPHERS

The sensor inside your digital camera is designed to work within a whole range of lighting conditions, and it's here where knowing about your camera's ISO settings comes in handy. Taking control of your camera's ISO – which regulates its sensitivity to light – allows you to choose the most appropriate option for the scene in hand. By doing so, you can ensure that images captured in good light retain excellent image quality, while those captured in sub-optimum conditions still emerge sharp and full of detail. Problems arise at higher sensitivities where the camera tries to produce the best images it can with the light available, and also at longer exposures, but the good news is that your camera will typically have tools at its disposal to counter these effects. So, what options are there, and exactly when should you use them?

TRY TO FIND A NEW WAY TO SHOOT ICONIC SIGHTS LIKE MT FUJI IN JAPAN.

Don't forget to shoot portraits of the locals, such as this Masai tribesman.

Keep a look-out for interesting close-up details, like this car in Havava, Cuba.

CUBA
BO247P

CLASSIC LANDSCAPE VIEWS, SUCH AS THIS ONE OF BAVENO, ITALY, LOOK BEST IN EARLY MORNING OR LATE AFTERNOON.

Seek out subjects that reveal something of the local culture, such as this shop front in Arles, France.

SHOOTING TIPS

• For some establishing shots of the city or locality, try an early morning trip to a high viewpoint such as the top of a hill. As well as wide views, use a telephoto lens to zoom in on prominent landmarks or interesting sections of your wide view.

• Choose the right time of day to visit landmarks, when the light is best. In many cases you'll get a more interesting shot if you step back and include some local hustle and bustle in the foreground, rather than just an empty record shot of the landmark itself.

• Cultures are about people as well as the places they live in. Shoot lots of portraits. These can be a mix of candid shots and posed pictures. Outdoor markets are always a good place to go. Many locals will be wise to photographers and expect payment to have their pictures taken, so take some change. The danger is you'll get a hackneyed pose rather than a natural shot – in some cases you'll get better shots if you shoot first and pay later. On the whole, being open and friendly is a better approach than sneaking around surreptitiously.

• Look out for detail shots that say something about the culture you're visiting, such as interesting signs, unusual food, window displays and so forth. Crop in close on the subject, perhaps in combination with a wide aperture to blur the background.

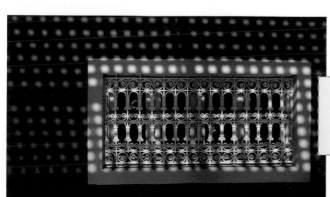

Light and colour were the main attractions of this detail In Marrakesh, Morocco.

CHAPTER FIVE

PORTRAITS »

PEOPLE AND PORTRAITS

WHAT'S THE MOST POPULAR PHOTOGRAPHIC SUBJECT IN THE WORLD? PEOPLE. GETTING GREAT PORTRAITS IS EASIER THAN YOU MAY THINK

Everyone likes to photograph their family and friends, but most people pictures are casual snaps. With a little knowledge and extra effort, it's not that difficult to create portraits that are more aesthetically pleasing and that reveal a glimpse of the subject's personality.

INDOOR PORTRAITS

The average home provides many potentially good portrait settings. An armchair, sofa, bed or the dining room table can all be pressed into service. Use the natural light of a window or conservatory, or use an off-camera flashgun. Avoid direct on-camera flash as your main light source – it's ugly and kills any atmosphere that may be present. Bouncing a flashgun off an adjacent white wall, or the ceiling, provides more flattering illumination. Have a quick tidy up before the shoot to ensure that any empty mugs and the like have been cleared away, or they'll be a distraction.

OUTDOOR PORTRAITS

Outdoors there is more light and a greater choice of settings. Avoid direct sun – a cloudy day is best, or open shade, where the light is even on the face. Avoid having the subject look towards the sun, which will make them squint. Shooting into the sun, on the other hand, can produce an appealing 'rim light' around the subject's edges, but you'll need either a reflector or flash to light the face, and take care with your exposure.

For the most flattering portraits use a short telephoto lens (around 50-100mm on a typical APS-C DSLR is ideal), and use a wide aperture to blur the background. This will make the subject stand out from their surroundings.

Alternatively go in close with a wideangle lens, like many photojournalists. This can add drama, impact and attitude, which suits certain types of shot.

When posing your subject, look for a setting that allows them to do more than just stand and gawp into the camera – perhaps a wall or some steps to sit on, or a doorway, tree or lamp post to lean against.

PHOTOGRAPHING KIDS

The best pictures of children are often candids when they're unaware of the camera, or are acting spontaneously. Catching them engaged in an activity is often a better approach than just getting them to say cheese into the camera.

You can get good posed shots, too, but keep sessions brief to avoid bored expressions. Another approach is to frame them unawares and then call their attention. You've then got just a few seconds to catch a spontaneous smile.

Get down to the kids' level rather than looking down on them. As with all portraits, get in close and fill the frame if you can. If they're fairly static you can zoom in on them so you can stay at a discreet distance, but if they're running around it may be better to get in close with a wideangle lens and mid-range aperture which will give a sense of being in the thick of the action, and increases your chances of getting them in focus.

GROUP PHOTOS

For a formal group shot, have the subjects turn their bodies so they're facing in towards the centre of the image, and arrange them so that their heads are at different heights. With larger groups place them in rows rather than a long line. For a more fun perspective, try shooting from low down with a wideangle, with your subjects all looking down at you.

POSING TIPS

There are no hard and fast rules for portraits, but here are a few tips to consider.

• Shoot from just above eye level: Shooting from slightly above your subject's eyes avoids the unflattering prospect of looking up their nostrils!

• Turn the body at an angle: Standing square on to the camera can often look creatively dull and generally unflattering. Turn the body at an angle to the camera, even if the head is facing the lens.

• Hands: Hands can often look awkward. If the subject finds a natural position that looks okay then fine. Otherwise try giving the hands something to do – holding something, wrapped around a knee, or resting a head in them, for example. If in doubt, crop in tighter and exclude them from the shot.

SHOOTING AT CLOSE RANGE WITH A WIDEANGLE LENS CAN CREATE IMPACT.

Spontaneous, unposed shots of children are usually the best.

INDOOR PORTRAITS

DON'T LET THE WEATHER BE ANY BARRIER TO YOUR PHOTOGRAPHY. TURN YOUR HOME INTO A TEMPORARY STUDIO TO GET SOME GREAT PORTRAITS

Okay, so the weather is grotty outside, but you want to shoot portraits. Why not convert your home (or someone else's) into a temporary home studio. You could move all the furniture out of the way and hang up a white background, but why not use the environment that's there and go for a more natural result? Alternatively find an interesting public building or office to shoot in.

Try using the furniture and props in the room to make the subject look relaxed and comfortable. There are lots of posing possibilities even with something as simple as a sofa. Architectural details such as window ledges and staircases have lots of potential too.

With indoor portraits, lighting is key. If you can shoot near a window, that's the best option. A north-facing one will give you soft diffused light whatever the weather outside. Use reflectors to mould the light and fill in the shadow areas.

If you don't have windows, or prefer not to use them, then you can create your own lighting using either flashguns or studio lighting – studio flash or tungsten-based lighting kits have never been so affordable – and have total control over the final result. For example, you can create high-key or low-key lighting effects just by your choice of background and lighting style.

LOW KEY

Low-key images are primarily dark or even completely black, punctuated with highlights to complete images with extended contrast. To achieve this effect choose a dark background and light your subject with a single, directional light-source, ensuring that no light spills onto the background. Both high-key and low-key images work especially well with black and white, as well as colour.

HIGH KEY

A high-key image is one composed primarily of highlight tones. To achieve this look, choose a light subject and a light background, use soft light to avoid deep shadows, then overexpose to make your shadows midtones, and your midtones highlights. This technique works great with portraits.

High-key images are mainly composed of light tones. Choose light clothing and backgrounds and use soft lighting to avoid deep shadows.

USE THE AVAILABLE FURNITURE AS PROPS TO CREATE A NATURAL PORTRAIT. BEDS ARE GOOD — THEY'RE COMFORTABLE AND OFFER LOTS OF POSING OPTIONS.

LOW-KEY IMAGES ARE MOSTLY MADE UP OF DARK TONES. DARK BACKGROUNDS AND DIRECTIONAL LIGHTING ARE THE KEY ELEMENTS HERE. CREATE AREAS OF DEEP SHADOW AND EXPOSE TO RECORD THE LIT AREAS AS MIDTONES.

Indoor Portraits

OUTDOOR PORTRAITS

THE WORLD IS YOUR STUDIO WHEN YOU SHOOT OUTSIDE, AND YOU HAVE AN INFINITE VARIETY OF BACKGROUNDS, PROPS AND LIGHTING

You don't need a studio to shoot portraits – the great outdoors provides an infinite variety of picture-making opportunities. But there are many pitfalls to be avoided if you want to achieve success.

The first is to beware of direct sun. Cloudy days are great because the light is soft and even, with no harsh shadows. On sunny days a shady spot will provide even light. Alternatively, step out into the sun but turn the subject so that they have their back to it. This stops them squinting, and will also bathe their face in diffused, reflected light rather than harsh sunlight.

This type of backlighting can add a halo of light around the subject which looks great,

especially with long hair. Meter from the subject's face so your exposure isn't influenced by light from behind them. You may want to use a reflector to direct more light onto the face.

To relax your subject use the natural environment as props. Find a tree or some other nearby element for them to hold or lean on. Architectural settings such as doorways and steps can make excellent locations, and be integrated into the composition.

Alternatively go for simplicity by using a plain wall, or an open spot in the park with just a blurred, distant backdrop.

Unless you're intending to show some of the environment, a short telephoto lens set to a fairly wide aperture provides the most flattering perspective of your subject, and also throws the background into a blur so it doesn't distract.

If you're photographing children, or seated adults, it's best to crouch down and shoot from a lower angle to avoid looking down on them too much. Just above eye level is a good rule of thumb.

SHOOTING OUTDOORS GIVES THE OPPORTUNITY TO USE AVAILABLE BACKGROUNDS AND PROPS TO CREATE A NATURAL, REALISTIC PORTRAIT THAT DOESN'T LOOK POSED.

OUTDOOR PORTRAITS

A plain wall in the shade of a railway station platform gave a perfect setting for this portrait. It was taken using a standard 50mm lens.

BY TURNING THE SUBJECT SO THE SUN WAS BEHIND HER, THE FACE IS BATHED IN SOFT LIGHT, THERE IS NO SQUINTING AND THERE'S A LOVELY HIGHLIGHT ON THE HAIR. A TELEPHOTO LENS AND WIDE APERTURE HAS THROWN THE BACKGROUND NICELY OUT OF FOCUS TOO.

Outdoor Portraits

ENVIRONMENTAL PORTRAITS

This man working at a Jaipur carpet factory made an interesting shot. Shooting into the light lit up the wool and made an attractive as well as informative background, but a dash of fill flash was required to light the subject.

SOMETIMES IT'S MORE INTERESTING TO STEP BACK OR ZOOM OUT A BIT AND SHOW PEOPLE IN THEIR SURROUNDINGS, OR ENGAGED IN AN ACTIVITY

Not all posed portraits need to be close-up head and shoulders shots. In fact often you may want to step back a bit and show the setting too. This helps to give the person some context and can tell the viewer something about where the person lives, or what they do for a living, or what their hobby is. A fisherman shown sat on the river bank next to his keep net, and the waterway snaking off into the distance, may well make a better picture than a closely cropped portrait.

People are often more happy to be photographed with something that they're proud

of or that's important to them, and are likely to feel a little more relaxed and comfortable when you're shooting from slightly further away.

For this type of portraiture you're most likely to want to use a relatively short focal length lens – either a standard or wideangle – otherwise you'll have to shoot from some distance away. With very wide angle lenses beware of distortion, especially towards the edges of the frame, when your subject's head could take on an elliptical shape, but remember that you can use the perspective effect to place a relevant part of

the setting in the foreground and, in doing so, give it extra emphasis. If the person is in the foreground they will become the dominant subject, while the setting will take a secondary background role.

You can shoot environmental portraits indoors or out, but the latter has the advantage of being easier from a lighting point of view, although the usual rules apply about choosing the quality and direction of light carefully. Indoors a high ISO or some fill flash may be required.

This Calcutta craftsman makes straw figures for festivals and events. A 10-20mm wideangle lens was used to show him at work, with the fruits of his labours trailing away behind him.

THIS PORTRAIT OF A WAITER IN A FIVE-STAR HOTEL IS GIVEN MORE CONTEXT BY THE INCLUSION OF HIS WORKPLACE BEHIND HIM.

The interior of a bicycle shop in Calcutta. The owner is relatively small in the frame, surrounded by his bikes and paraphernalia.

CANDID PORTRAITS

WHEN PEOPLE ARE AWARE OF THE CAMERA THEY CHANGE THEIR DEMEANOUR. SHOOT UNOBSERVED FOR MORE NATURAL IMAGES OF PEOPLE AND LIFE

Many reportage and travel photographers like to shoot candid shots of people going about their lives, especially if they're doing something interesting, because as soon as they become aware of the camera people often freeze up, and become self-conscious and, well, a bit wooden. People are obviously at their most natural when they don't know they're being observed.

This kind of photography is more difficult than it used to be because people and authorities are a lot more paranoid about photography, and attitudes towards photographing children have also changed in recent years, so it's best to stick to adult subjects. There are, however, a few tricks that you can use to increase your chances of getting intriguing 'slice of life' shots without being observed.

LENS CHOICE

Many people assume that to shoot unobserved you need to stand some distance away with a long telephoto lens. While this is still an option it's by no means the only way to do it, and you can also get great shots, unseen, from close range with a wideangle if you employ the right technique. The most important thing is not to stand with your camera pressed up against your face for long periods because people will spot you. Keep the camera by your side, pre-set your exposure and ISO for the conditions and just observe, casually, the scene around you. At the right moment raise the camera to your eye, compose and shoot and lower the camera again. The entire operation can be done in about two seconds. Then repeat as necessary. If you're quick your subject won't notice even if they're just a couple of metres from you. If your camera makes noises, such as focus confirmation bleeps, then turn these off first.

You can also try pointing the camera at something adjacent to your intended subject, keeping your other eye discreetly on your target, then quickly pan round and click at the right moment.

If you're using a long lens, or the panning technique, you'll need to pre-set a shutter speed that's fast enough to avoid camera shake.

THE WAIST-LEVEL APPROACH

Many modern digital cameras feature tilt and swivel LCD screen and these can be great for candid photography. By keeping the camera at waist level but tilting the screen upwards you can see your composition without lifting the camera. Try finding a seat and resting the camera discreetly on your thigh.

With the right technique you can shoot candids even with a standard lens.

TELEPHOTO LENSES ENABLE YOU TO CAPTURE CAPTIVATING SCENES WITHOUT BEING OBSERVED. THESE PICTURES WERE TAKEN USING A 70–300MM ZOOM.

CHAPTER SIX

PHOTO PROJECTS »

4 IDEAS FOR THE WEEKEND

IF YOU'RE LOOKING FOR A CREATIVE CHALLENGE TO INSPIRE YOUR PHOTOGRAPHY THIS WEEKEND, THEN LOOK NO FURTHER. HERE WE HAVE FOUR VERY DIFFERENT BUT EQUALLY EXCITING PROJECTS FOR YOU TO SINK YOUR TEETH IN — AND A COUPLE OF GREAT DAYS OUT TO ENJOY AT THE SAME TIME!

SHOOT BLOSSOM FROM AN UNUSUAL ANGLE

We know spring is well and truly here when colourful petals finally arrive on the cherry blossom trees. Now is the time to make the most of them, so try something different by capturing their beauty from a more unusual angle. What we want you to do is photograph the blooms from below, framed against a blue sky.

The contrast between the delicate and brightly coloured petals and the blue background will work really well.

In Japan, cherry blossom trees symbolise clouds because they bloom and change so quickly. There are over 100 different kinds of blossom tree, and many grow here in the UK. Some can have up to 100 petals per flower, and they come in an array of colours and can bloom for up to four weeks – plenty of time to find and shoot them then!

You need a location that is easy to access – somewhere you can stand pretty much underneath the trees. You'll also need a bright sunny day so the skies are a bold blue colour. It's best to use a clear sky too. One or two clouds won't distract from the blossom, but an overcast day definitely will. When you're there, point your camera up to the branches and lean back so your camera tilts towards the sky. Zoom in on the end of a branch so the frame is filled with just blossom and blue sky, and try not to let one element overpower the other. Then carefully focus on the blossom, as it's important we see every last detail. Get it right and you'll have a simple and delicate floral masterpiece to hang on your wall.

HOW TO TAKE YOUR IMAGE

1 CHOOSE YOUR SETTINGS

Switch to aperture-priority and select an aperture of around f/4 to ensure the background is out of focus. Focus on the models' LCD screen and switch to spot metering to ensure the LCD is metered for.

4 IDEAS FOR THE WEEKEND

2 COMPOSE YOUR IMAGE

Composition is really important, so if you have Live View use it. Make sure the models' LCD is prominent in the frame and position yourself so your models and location can still be seen clearly in the background.

BRIGHT IDEA

Check out the 'What's on' guide on your local council's website for a list of festivals and events near you.

DOCUMENT A SUMMER FÊTE

Nothing says community spirit like going to the local village or town fête. And with the sunshine making more appearances now, weekends will be packed with them. These local events are great examples of how communities come together to have fun, and it's the perfect opportunity to capture your neighbourhood's spirit.

Use a standard lens so you can capture portraits and wider scenes too. Go with a friend so you feel more comfortable taking pictures, and start with a local event – knowing a few faces will make it easier. There will be shots everywhere, from people devouring cupcakes to kids running the egg and spoon race with freshly painted faces. Be chatty and friendly when you approach people, and don't be afraid to ask if you want them to pose for you. Afterwards, why not organise your images into a book?

4 IDEAS FOR THE WEEKEND

EYE SPY WITH MY LITTLE EYE...

...something beginning with magnifying glass! This is a quick and easy way to give your portraits that extra 'oomph', and all you need is a magnifying glass. Not only do our eyes give us one of our most vital senses, they're also the key focal point of any portrait. What we're asking you to do is take a portrait as you would normally, but this time ask your model to hold a magnifying glass over one of their eyes and look directly at the camera. Their eye will appear giant-sized! The magnifying glass should be no smaller than the eye and needs to be held 20-30cm away from them. Focus on the glass and the enlarged eye (rather than the model's actual eye) and avoid using flash, as this could produce glare on the glass.

The magnifying glass will be the closest point to the camera so if you set an aperture of around f/11 then the model should be in sharp focus too. Try using extra props like bowler hats or fake moustaches to add more character to your images, and turn your model into a detective!

4 IDEAS FOR THE WEEKEND

CREATE A STILL LIFE AT THE SEASIDE

Pebbles, shells, buckets, spades... there are all kinds of still life subjects to shoot on the beach. And sand will make for a perfect backdrop, because there's plenty of it and it's easy to change – it can be smoothed over, darkened or mucked up again in minutes. When it comes to arranging subjects, attention to detail is key. Minimise distractions, and try arranging the objects into shapes and lines to make them stand out even more – make pebbles into footprints, seashells into animals, or buckets into giant faces.

When it's time to shoot, step back and avoid treading near the subjects, as you don't want footprints ruining a background. Shoot down onto the scene to avoid distortion and avoid unwanted distractions like towels and deckchair legs. Get high above the subjects by standing on your tiptoes and leaning in, or find a sturdy fold-out chair or coolbox. Then when you're done, simply rearrange the subjects and shoot away again. Have fun at the beach!

WINTER PROJECTS

10 PROJECT IDEAS TO KEEP YOU BUSY ALL WINTER

IDEA 1 SHOOT AN OUTDOOR WINTER PORTRAIT

WHY:

Grab your faux fur-lined coat – it's the perfect time of year to shoot sub-Arctic people pictures. Just make sure you wrap up warm too!

When friends and family are wrapped up in hats, scarves and furry coats, take advantage of the situation and shoot a wintertime portrait. Just because it's cold outside, it doesn't mean that you should avoid outdoor portraiture like the plague. Yes noses and cheeks can be a little rosy, but don't see this as a problem because it's quite natural and typical of the season.

To shoot a portrait like this you don't need any special gear at all. Just a kit lens or a medium telephoto will do the job perfectly. If you're shooting on an 18-55mm kit lens, or even an 18-105mm, zoom into the longest focal length. This will give you a reasonable working distance where you're not too close to the model. If you're going for a tight composition like our example, ask the model to hold the collar of their jacket or to bunch their scarf under their chin. This helps to create lead-in lines to the face, which is framed by a hat and scarf or furry hood. If you decide to go for a wider composition you could still use this pose, but with the background in the shot you have to be much more careful about what's behind the model. Bushes and evergreen trees can produce pleasing and natural backgrounds for this type of portrait.

In terms of camera settings, set ISO to around 400, lower it to 100 if it's a bright day and possibly higher to 800 if it's really dull. Shoot in aperture-priority with the aperture set to around f/5.6. This is often the maximum aperture for kit lenses at full zoom and will make obtaining sharp shots easier than when shooting with wider apertures. Shutter speed will be taken care of by the camera, but keep an eye on it and make sure it doesn't become so slow that camera shake becomes a problem. So what are you waiting for? Grab a coat, hat and scarf and get shooting.

QUICK TIP:

A reflector can be a great way to lighten shadows, even when light levels are low. When your model is wearing a hat or hood, you'd be surprised at how much light is blocked from the face.

KEEP WARM OUTSIDE

There's nothing worse than being cold and miserable on a shoot, which is why it's so important to wear suitable clothing.

WINTER ACCESSORIES

Hats, gloves, scarves, arm warmers, ear muffs... the list of winter warmers goes on! Ask your model to wear a few of these to add to the winter feel of your portrait.

ADD MORE LIGHT

Use a reflector to bounce light onto the model's face. This will soften any harsh shadows and add natural highlights, giving your model a flattering glow.

IDEA 2 GET CREATIVE WITH WHITE BALANCE

WHY:

Warm up, or indeed cool down, your winter landscapes for more creative results. It's easy to do and takes only a matter of seconds in Raw.

Winter light is most often considered to be much warmer than that in spring, summer and autumn because of the low position of the sun in the sky. However, it's also not uncommon for light to be cold with a bluish tint. In this situation you may want to warm shots up by increasing the amount of yellow tint.

Conversely, cooling down an exceptionally warm shot to make it appear more neutral may be necessary. To change the colour balance of your Raw shots, all you need to do is move the Color Temperature slider at the top of the Adobe Raw and Lightroom controls. This slider controls the blue and yellow tint in images – drag it to the left and it increases blue to cool photos down, drag it right and it warms shots up by increasing yellow. Move the slider slowly and keep an eye on the effect in the main

image window. If you're not happy with the result and want to start again from the original white balance, go to the dropdown menu that will now be set to Custom, and choose As Shot. Once you're happy with the result and have done all the other processing, export your image as normal.

QUICK TIP:

Winter light is softer than in the summer because the sun is lower in the sky, but on cloudy days this can mean light levels are quite low. Set ISO 400-800 for usable exposures.

CHOOSE LOWEST ISO
For the best possible image quality, always select your lowest ISO setting. This shot was taken at ISO 50, though ISO 100 is the lowest on many DSLRs and CSCs.

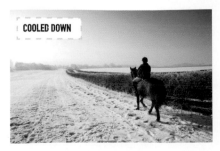
COOLED DOWN

WARMED UP

123

WINTER PROJECTS

ENSURE SHARP SHOTS
If you're using a wide focal length between 10-30mm, an aperture of f/8-f/11 will be enough to ensure front-to-back sharpness. Focus one-third into the scene.

METER FOR HIGHLIGHTS
Crisp snow is incredibly reflective, so you will need to meter carefully to ensure detail in the highlights. Use exposure compensation to ensure correct exposure.

IDEA 3 SHOOT A WINTER LANDSCAPE

WHY:

You can only shoot a frosty or snow-covered landscape in winter – be prepared for it and get out shooting when the weather is just right.

Frost and snow can make ordinary scenes extraordinary. You wake up in the morning to find everything covered in glistening ice, beckoning you outside with your DSLR. There's no time to wait – pull on your boots and get out shooting as soon as possible before the snow or ice melts. When shooting snow you need to take control of exposure to ensure that it isn't captured as a dull grey. A predominance of light tones, like white, in any scene will always fool the camera into underexposure, so you'll always need to use exposure compensation in this situation. It's difficult to say exactly how much because different situations, weather conditions and light will always be a determining factor. Start off by taking a shot in aperture-priority with 1 stop of overexposure and check the result on the LCD. If this looks good then continue with this setting; if not, dial in one more stop and take another test shot. Generally speaking, you'll always need between 1 and 2 stops of overexposure to ensure your snowy shots are correctly exposed and your snow is actually white.

QUICK TIP:

Shoot Raw to ensure that no detail is lost. Highlight recovery is very effective, but if you shoot JPEG detail could be lost forever.

IDEA 4 CREATE QUIRKY STILL LIFES

WHY?

Because mince pies aren't just for eating!

If it's too cold for landscapes, turn your attention indoors. After all, nothing says winter like boiling hot chocolate and roasted marshmallows. Plus, you've got all the Christmas extras like tinsel, fairy lights and brightly wrapped presents. So why not create a still life that captures the season's iconic quirks without having to wrap up like an Eskimo. And you don't even have to leave your kitchen!

Use your worktop as a mini studio and use either natural light if you're close to a window, or a desktop lamp if it's dark outside. You could even use candlelight to create a warm, wintry feel – just make sure you use a tripod, as shutter speeds will be much slower. If your worktop has seen better days, use a plain piece of paper or card to create a spotless infinity curve.

Out-of-focus fairy lights can bring simple setups to life. They provide pleasing highlights without distracting from the main subject, while adding to the festive mood. Try using different coloured cellophane over lights too.

QUICK TIP:

You could try shaping the out-of-focus highlights – see idea 6 to find out how.

IDEA 6 SHAPE YOUR OUT-OF-FOCUS HIGHLIGHTS

WHY?

You can create unique results and have great fun along the way.

Did you know that you could shape your bokeh (the blurred areas of your photos) by simply cutting shapes into card? Well, you can, and the results can be truly amazing. Stars, hearts, even Christmas trees and holly... so long as you can quickly and easily cut it out, you can use it. All you need to get started is some black card, a craft knife and some Blu-Tack.

Draw around your lens cap to create the basic shape of your template, and then carefully draw and cut out your shape right in the middle of the circle. Just make sure it's no bigger than a 2p piece, otherwise the shape loses clarity. Don't be too clever with the shape either – it's really best to keep it simple. And be generous when you cut out the template too, as you want it to be slightly larger than the actual lens otherwise light might creep in around the sides.

Use Blu-Tack to stick the template over the end of your lens, then select the widest available aperture you can – typically f/4 or f/2.8 – and point your lens directly at a light source like our fairy lights. Carefully focus on your main subject (or, if you're shooting an abstract, deliberately defocus on the lights) and shoot away!

PHOTO CHALLENGE:

Cut your name into a template and create your own very personalised highlights.

WITHOUT BOKEH TEMPLATE

WITH BOKEH TEMPLATE

TRY DIFFERENT SHAPES

We tried cutting out stars, Christmas trees, and even a plane. So long as your shapes are small and simple, they'll work just fine for this bokeh effect.

COLOURFUL ABSTRACTS

MAKING MINI LENSES OUT OF WATER DROPLETS IS SO EASY WITH THIS QUICK, EASY AND COLOURFUL DIY MACRO PROJECT. FOLLOW OUR TECHNIQUE TODAY FOR STUNNING RESULTS ON A SHOESTRING!

You don't need a fancy studio or an expensive macro lens to create interesting still lifes at home. This effect is easily achieved by creating lots of tiny water droplets on a sheet of glass, which is suspended above colourful objects. By using a narrow depth-of-field and focusing on the droplets, the background is thrown out of focus, but because the droplets act like tiny lenses, an in-focus image of the background can be seen in each droplet in surprising detail.

Not only is this a quick and easy project, it also only requires a few low-cost items. Firstly, you'll need a pane of glass. One out of a picture frame would be perfect, and while A3 works best you can get away with A4. You'll also need some windscreen cleaner to treat your glass with, so that the water beads on the surface. You can buy some from your local supermarket or auto store. It's very important that you make sure the cleaner has beading properties, or the droplets will spread out on the glass surface making it difficult to achieve the desired effect.

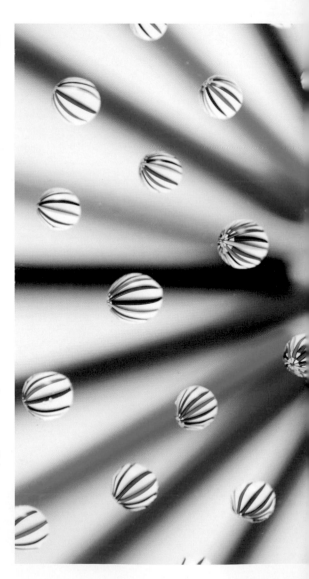

The subject under the glass should be colourful and recognisable, so it's easily identifiable through the droplets. For our shot we arranged coloured pencils into a spiral on some white paper. We removed the darker coloured pencils as they weren't bright enough for the shot. We then used a drinking straw to pipette the droplets onto the glass.

We used a standard 24-70mm lens and zoomed in nice and close to the droplets. If you want to zoom in even more a macro lens is ideal, but our lens took a lovely final image. Shoot in aperture-priority so you can control your depth-of-field, and use f/5.6 to start. The background needs to be out of focus but not too blurred. Take your time with this project because

every detail matters – from arranging your colourful subject, creating the droplets, and then focusing on them. But once you get stuck in, you'll be thinking of all kinds of objects to photograph under this maze of droplets.

QUICK TIP

Colourful subjects like Skittles also make great subjects under the glass. They're mesmerising to look at!

NOW SET UP YOUR HOME STUDIO FOR FUNKY STILL LIFES

Got a spare hour or two? Then it's time to scout around for the items to create this budget-busting technique.

The things you'll need...

- ✓ Plain white paper
- ✓ Colourful subject(s)
- ✓ A3/A4 glass pane
- ✓ Support for the glass pane
- ✓ Windscreen cleaner
- ✓ Glass of water
- ✓ Drinking straws
- ✓ Kitchen towel – in case of any accidental spillages!

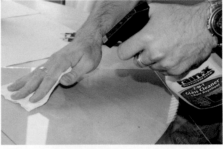

1 BUILD A MINI STUDIO

Find an area of your home with plenty of natural light. Cover your surface with plain white paper, and arrange your coloured pencils in the middle. Suspend a glass pane between two supports that are 20-25cm tall.

2 CLEAN YOUR GLASS

Pick up the glass and clean it thoroughly with your rain-repellant windscreen cleaner, which can be bought from a supermarket. This is essential, as without it the water won't bead into droplets.

3 CREATE A DROPLET

Reposition the glass. Dip your straw in a glass of water and remove, keeping a finger over the end. Squeeze the straw to release a droplet. Keep the straw very close to the glass surface for perfect droplets.

4 FILL THE FRAME AREA

Taking care to space them evenly, begin covering the surface of the glass with droplets. Make sure you know where the corners of your frame will be so you have enough coverage when you come to shoot.

5 COMPOSE AND SHOOT

Take your shots from directly above the glass pane so that all of the droplets are in focus. You may have to focus manually. Good luck!